WEEKEND LOG CABIN QUILTS

FOR PEOPLE WHO DON'T HAVE TIME TO QUILT

PLUS

LOTS OF VARIATIONS

by Marti Michell

BOOK THREE OF THE
"QUILTING FOR PEOPLE
WHO DON'T HAVE TIME TO QUILT" SERIES

Featuring:	Quilt Designs included:
No Pattern Pieces	Log Cabin
Strip and Chain Piecing	Pineapple
Quilt-As-You-Sew Invisible Machine Quilting	Linked Chevrons
Traditional Machine Quilting	& other Log Cabin Variations

WELCOME TO OUR CABIN

The Log Cabin Quilt and its derivatives have been extremely popular quilt designs since they first appeared in the mid-1800s. Surely one of the reasons is that making the individual block is unique, intriguing and at the same time, easy. But, best of all, the Log Cabin looks difficult and complicated, which in turn allows the quiltmaker to look like a genius.

The Weekend Log Cabin technique speeds up the process, so now making Log Cabins is easy, fun, **and** quick. With the Quilt-As-You-Sew techniques you will learn in this book, you really **can** complete a Log Cabin quilt in a single weekend. Be warned, however, once you get started it could be habit forming. Just so you won't get bored, we have included enough variations and ideas to last forever!

Just what is Quilt-As-You-Sew? In traditional quilting, the quiltmaker pieces each block, assembles the blocks into a quilt top, pins or bastes the quilt top to the batting and backing, and only then begins to quilt. Some quiltmakers rearrange the process by piecing the blocks, quilting each one individually (eliminating the need for a frame), and then assembling the quilted blocks. This process is sometimes called quilt-as-you-**go**. But the Quilt-As-You-**Sew** technique is even easier and faster!

In Quilt-As-You-Sew, you actually quilt the blocks at the same time as you assemble them. Borders can be attached Quilt-As-You-Sew as well. The best thing about the Quilt-As-You-Sew method is that it results in completed quilts, not just tops! No quilt frame is needed, no time wasted wondering how to use a quilt frame. Time-consuming handwork is reduced to a minimum. Beautiful quilts to use or share can be yours in less time than you ever dreamed.

It's not that I don't like hand quilting or hand-quilted quilts, it's just that I am realistic about the amount of time that I have. Also, I happen to enjoy the patchwork process and the fun of putting fabrics together more than the quilting process. The productivity of this method allows quilts to become real gift items, because the amount of time you have invested is minimal.

If you've never made a hand-quilted quilt, you may not understand that most people who give a hand-quilted quilt continue to refer to it as "my quilt". They don't go to visit the recipient, they go to check on the quilt!

Today, I am in love with machine quilting and it's okay for machine quilting to be seen. Some days, the more it shows and sparkles with metallic threads and becomes an integral part of the quilt, the happier I am. But in an earlier stage of my quilting life, I wouldn't machine quilt if it could be seen on the top side of the quilt. I went to great lengths to develop techniques for hidden machine quilting. That was when this method for Quilt-As-You-Sew first surfaced. I'm glad I went through that period, because this is a wonderful technique.

Not all the quilts included in this book were made Quilt-As-You-Sew. You will learn that this technique is most suited for quilts with a moderate number of relatively large Log Cabin blocks. Those quilts which are not made Quilt-As-You-Sew are not less fun to make; they simply take longer. The book gives instructions both for the Quilt-As-You-Sew method and traditional machine quilting. By incorporating machine quilting, all but two of the quilts in this book could be Weekend Log Cabins.

GETTING STARTED

Folklore attributes the Log Cabin name to the building it portrays. Just as the settlers built their cabins with interlocking logs around a central chimney, quilters construct a log cabin block with fabric "logs" around a center square "hearth." The center square is often red to suggest warmth and it usually remains the same size and color throughout the quilt. I have always been fascinated by the building procedure of the Log Cabin block. The block is assembled so that the pieces spiral around the center square in the order shown in **Fig A**. You start with the center square and work clockwise, attaching one strip of fabric at a time. As it happens, this order of construction is what makes the block so conducive to Quilt-As-You-Sew techniques.

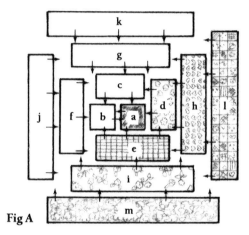

Fig A

The Log Cabin block is traditionally divided diagonally into light and dark halves. All the strips in one half of the block are light and the other half are dark, with a contrasting center square. The strips in one half are shorter than in the other. I like the blocks best with light fabrics – usually a more neutral color – in the half with the shorter strips. The emphasis on dark and light also makes the block especially conducive to scraps. The strong diagonal design line in each block allows very interesting arrangements for Log Cabin quilts. The arrangements of the blocks (the sets) are so distinctive that many of them have their own names; Barn Raising, Straight Furrows, Pinwheel, are examples.

As you can see by the photographs of the projects in this book, quilts with greatly differing looks can be made by simply varying the fabrics, "log" width, center square size, and the set of the blocks. Sometimes the center block is bigger than the width of the logs. This is, of course, an easy way to make the entire block bigger without adding another round of strips. But I generally prefer a center square the same dimension as the strips and a darker color (as in the basic *Country Christmas* quilt block), so that perfect "stair steps" diagonally divide the block.

There Are No Pattern Pieces

When making Log Cabin quilts, there is no need for pattern pieces. Besides the center square, all the pieces are strips. The only measurements you need to know to make these quilts are how big the center square of each individual block is and how wide the strips are. Everything else is done automatically as you piece. The size of the first strip you cut determines the scale of the quilt and the finished size of the block.

The measurements are in inches and yards. Please use this conversion chart for centimeters and meters.

    1 meter = 39.37 inches
    1 inch = 2.54 cms
    yards x .9144 = meters
    inches x 2.54 = cms

It is especially helpful with Log Cabin quilts to make sure you know these geometric terms.

Diagonal - Extending at a slant between opposite corners, **Fig B**.

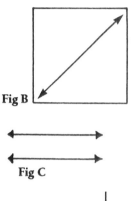

Fig B

Parallel - lines extending in the same direction at the same distance apart so as to never meet, **Fig C**.

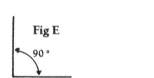

Fig C

Perpendicular - a straight line at right angles to another straight line, **Fig D**.

Fig D

Right Angle - a 90 degree angle - also called a square corner, **Fig E**.

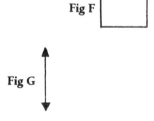

Fig E

90°

Square - a four sided figure having all of its sides equal length and all of its corners right angles, **Fig F**.

Fig F

Vertical - straight up and down, **Fig G**.

Fig G

Horizontal - parallel to the horizon, perpendicular to vertical, straight across, **Fig H**.

Fig H

Lengthwise - in the same direction as the length, **Fig I**.

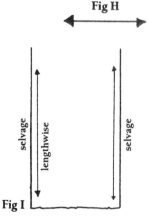

selvage   lengthwise   selvage

Fig I

Fabric Selection

Fabric selection is very important. It does much more to set the mood of the quilt than the pattern. Because most people aren't used to combining lots of different fabrics, the tendency for beginners is to overmatch everything and end up with border-line boring quilts.

Most quilters prefer 100% cotton fabrics. Any fabric can be used if you understand the consequences. For now, I would recommend 100% cotton.

Keeping in mind the importance of light and dark to the definition of the block is very important as you select fabrics. At the same time, you will want to look for a variety in the scale and density of design in prints selected. Variety helps define the individual strips one from another.

Learn to stand back and look before you buy or cut the fabrics selected for a quilt. We all tend to select fabrics at no more than an arm's length. But we rarely look at the finished quilt from that distance. Instead, it is viewed from "across the room". The fabrics can look very different then.

Deciding on a Color Plan and Fabric Arrangement

Because of the uniqueness of the Log Cabin block, selecting fabrics presents new challenges. Study the color photographs to see what appeals to you. Almost all fabric combinations shown can be transferred to other size quilts.

1. Selection of a color combination can be as simple as using two contrasting fabrics in opposite halves of the block and a center square, see the drapery print and muslin quilt we named *Star Set Log Cabin*, photographed on page 22.

2. You can use a different fabric in each position of the block, but make all blocks identical. If you make identical blocks, you will get double strips of some fabrics when the blocks are arranged. If these strips happen to be particularly dark or bright or high contrast in any way, it can be very distracting.

If you want a lot of control, it is better to develop two master blocks like our very special *Kittens in the Garden*, shown on the front cover.

3. A popular choice is to use the same light fabric in each strip on the light side and randomly positioned assorted fabrics on the dark side. For an example see the *12 Block Crib Quilt*, page 23.

4. The block can be all random scraps, which is probably my personal favorite. This is nicer with thinner strips and more blocks. See the *Pinwheel Log Cabin Quilt*, page 21.

5. What I call the "L" method of arrangement is quite common. Every fabric is used twice in succession, making an "L" in that half of the block and requiring less fabrics per block than if each strip is different.

6. If you want to make a multicolored quilt, the easiest way is to pick a multicolored fabric that you love and has the balance of colors you want. It is especially nice if you think it would make a good border. Then select fabrics to coordinate. One of the advantages of a wide variety of fabrics is that the differences in color and texture optically disguise many mistakes.

7. Some quilts require several different blocks to get the desired result. See *Full Spectrum* on page 24, and *How Much is that Doggie in the Window?* on page 23.

Fig J   **Straight Furrows**   Fig K   **Barn Raising**

8. You may want to make copies of the empty blocks diagrams of Straight Furrows and Barn Raising and use colored pencils to develop a color plan, **Fig J** and **Fig K** (see page 4).

Selecting from a Personal Fabric Collection

If you have a personal fabric collection, I would recommend one of the random methods, because it will be easy to pull out a large variety of different fabrics and use just a little of each.

Selecting at the Store

If you are buying all the fabrics at once, you may want to use one of the less complicated color schemes. You can get a pretty good idea of how the fabrics will look together by looking at bolts standing on edge.

Keeping Organized in each Block

If you are planning the arrangement of fabrics, it is a good idea to make a block chart by attaching small pieces of the fabric to a copy of the quilt block, **Fig L**. For the block to work as intended, it is necessary to piece in the same direction on all the blocks. It is easy in the beginning stages to go the wrong direction without a chart. A word of warning, it is possible to go the wrong direction even **with** a chart. It is a must, therefore, to make the chart and keep it by the sewing machine. You will need to refer to it throughout the making of your blocks.

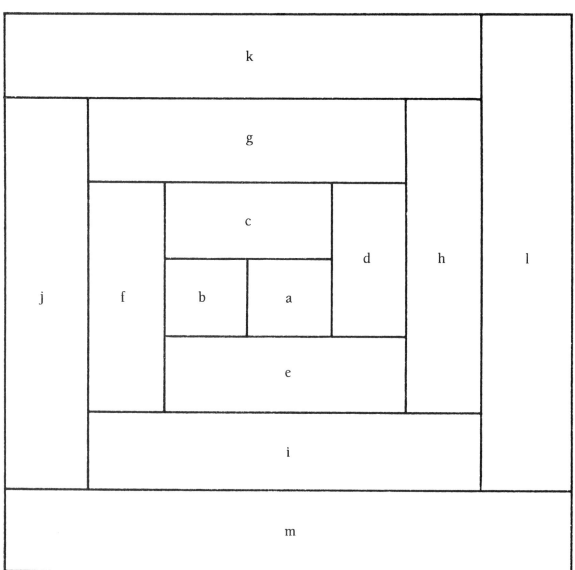

Fig L

Block Chart for planning fabric position

5

Backing Fabric for Quilt-As-You-Sew Quilts

Quilt-As-You-Sew quilts demand a separate piece of backing fabric for every block. If you want to camouflage this "block by block" technique, cut all the backing pieces from a single small random print. However, if you don't mind calling attention to this so-called "non-traditional" technique – and I don't – make the backs of your quilts interesting by cutting the block backs from all different fabrics. I make eye-catching quilt backs and use up leftover fabrics at the same time so I can buy new fabrics for tops! Try two different fabrics for the block backs, set them checkerboard style, and use a third fabric for the border backings and the seam covers. This is the approach used for the first project, the *Country Christmas Weekend Quilt*, page 10.

Backing Fabric for Machine-pieced Quilt Tops

Traditional quilt backs are usually made from one fabric with minimal piecing. A single 45-inch width of fabric will do for crib and wall quilts, but is too narrow for full-size quilts. Although most people piece two lengths for a full-size quilt with a lengthwise center seam, crosswise seams are okay.

Remember, there are no rules. These are quilts to make for fun, for using and for sharing. Sometimes people are surprised at some of the things I do for quiltmaking fun that they consider unorthodox. Whenever the "but that isn't the way **they** do it" attitude surfaces, I just reply, "I don't know who **they** are, but this is how I do it."

How Much Fabric Do I Need?

The question is, "How much do I need?" I have found that what I **need** and what I **want** are two different things. My policy has always been to buy as much as I could afford. Once you start making lots of quilts, you have a real appreciation for sewing from a stockpile of fabric. All of the quilts in this book made with assorted fabrics are more pleasing because I could easily increase the variety from my stockpile.

Just as there is no single fabric yardage requirement to make a dress, there is not one answer for how much fabric it takes to make a quilt. Here are some rules of thumb. Just the backing for a queen/double requires 6 1/2 yards. So, if you add fabric for seams and some latitude in cutting, I say you need a total of 10 yards for the surface of a not too complicated queen/double quilt. Following the same line of thought, a total of 12 1/2 yards for a king and 6 1/2 yards for a twin. Almost everyone agrees having extra is better than agonizing over running out. More and more I find I use my extra yardage for pieced backs for quilts or in pillow cases. I put them on top of the quilt propped against the bed, then I don't have to fight the pillow tuck battle.

The quilts shown do have estimated yardage requirements. All estimates used in this book are based on 45"-wide fabrics unless otherwise stated. Fat quarters (18" x 22 1/2"), available in many stores, are a nice way to purchase a small quantity of a wide variety of prints and still be able to cut a meaningful strip on the lengthwise grain (18").

Fabric Preparation

Contrary to nearly every article or book you have read, pre-washing your fabrics before using is not mandatory. My choice is to test my fabrics for shrinking and bleeding, but not to automatically pre-wash. I like the crispness of the fabric before it is washed. It is easier to use in the machine piecing and quilting techniques that I favor.

Since I start with strips anyway, I will cut a common size of strips, like 2" x 12", wet them completely in hot water, squeeze and iron dry. It is heat on the wet fiber that really causes the shrinkage. At the same time, I can look for any color bleeding. If any fabric bleeds or shrinks beyond the 2% to 3% allowed by industry standards, I pre-wash that fabric or select another fabric. 2% to 3% translates to 3/4" to 1" in a yard or 1/4" to 1/3" in 12". If one fabric shrinks considerably more than the others, it is a greater problem than if they all shrink the same little amount.

Batting Selection

The best batting for machine quilting and Quilt-As-You-Sew is a medium weight bonded polyester batting called all-purpose. Batting that is very thin just won't puff enough for this method. If it's too thick, it is difficult to work with. Look for batting which is bonded throughout, not just on the surface. Surface bonded batting can separate when washed. Look for a bonded batt that is reasonably soft, such as Hobbs Polydown®. Many of the battings sold on a roll in fabric stores are also suitable, just make sure they aren't stiff. Machine quilting is stiffer than hand quilting and a stiff batt results in a quilt that is too stiff.

The narrow width of most roll battings (usually 48") is not a problem for Quilt-As-You-Sew quilts (it has to be cut into small pieces anyway), traditional crib quilts or wall hangings. But for full-size non-Quilt-As-You-Sew quilts, you will need to piece the batting. To do so, butt the lengths together then sew them with a diagonal basting stitch.

Remove packaged batting from its bag a day or two ahead of time so it can relax. A careful steam press eliminates humps and bumps.

Tools

Accurate cutting is crucial. The rotary cutter system has really revolutionized the ease of making the Log Cabin Quilt. Some of my quiltmaking friends love the quilting most, some the piecing process, but I don't know anyone who loves the cutting. Yet accurate cutting is the first crucial step in accurate patchwork. One of the reasons the strip methods are so effective comes from the introduction of rotary cutting systems in the mid 1970s. The rotary cutter looks like an advanced pizza cutter. It must be used in conjunction with a special protective mat and is most effective with a rigid, thick acrylic ruler for long straight cuts!

With the rotary cutting method, you can be faster than with scissors, but more importantly, you can be more accurate than with scissors. You can accomplish the cutting processes outlined in this book with a ruler, pencil and scissors, but you'll save time measuring, save time cutting, and be more accurate with the rotary cutter method.

To be effective cutting strips with a rotary cutter, you need a strong straight edge. There are many different acrylic rulers 5" or 6" wide and 24" long. They are usually printed with a grid on the ruler surface that is very helpful in assuring accuracy. Most rulers also have angles and other special printed features.

With just a little practice, you'll be comfortable cutting nearly any straight line geometric shape with just a ruler and rotary cutter, further eliminating the need for patterns, templates, and tedious tracing. But for now, you only need to cut straight strips. Throughout the book, measurements are given in sizes for cutting.

Tips for Using the Rotary Cutter
The blades are very sharp. All of the brands currently available have guards. Make sure they are in place when the cutter is not in use. This protects both you and the blade. If you drop the cutter or accidentally cut across a pin, the blade often becomes nicked. Then instead of cutting the fabric where the blade is nicked, it perforates the fabric. The blades are replaceable, but the need can be minimized if you will just keep the guard in place. A fresh blade will cut 6 to 12 layers of fabric easily with very little pressure. Bearing down too hard is not necessary and can do irreparable damage to the protective mat. It's harder to accurately fold and stack 12 layers of fabric than to cut them. When cutting, the blade side, not the guard side, goes immediately next to the acrylic ruler. Cut away from you, not toward your body, **Fig M**.

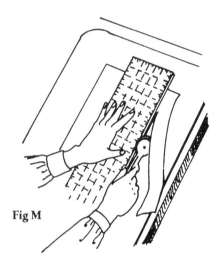

Fig M

To get straight strips, it is imperative that the ruler be perpendicular to the fold on folded fabrics and/or parallel to the selvage. The first cut is usually trimming off the selvage (if cutting strips on the lengthwise grain) or straightening a store cut edge (if cutting strips on the crosswise grain). To make a strip, the next cut is the second side of the first strip. It requires changing hands, going to the other side of the mat, or turning the mat. My favorite method is to cut the first strip left handed – not really hard with the good ruler – and the rest right handed which is my favored hand. Then I don't have to change table sides. Take advantage of the grids on the mat and on the ruler to maximize your accuracy.

Other Tools
Most other tools are probably already in your sewing supplies. Good small scissors, a seam ripper, thimbles, hand sewing needles, etc. You will probably want to add some specialized quilting tools like removable fabric marking pens and pencils, smaller acrylic rulers and squares. Put a steam iron and ironing board next to your sewing machine.

A small ruler or hem gauge to keep handy for double checking strip width and seam allowances is especially helpful for ensuring accuracy in the Log Cabin.

Your sewing machine doesn't have to be anything fancy. If you haven't used it recently, dust it off, oil it and change the needle. If the presser foot is pushing the layers out of alignment, you can usually correct that by reducing the pressure on the presser foot. (See your sewing machine manual for instructions.) If you have an even-feed attachment, you may want to use it.

Cutting the Fabrics and Batting
Some people use templates and cut the center square and each strip for the Log Cabin Block individually. You can do that, but cutting strips is faster, easier, and almost always more accurate. It is certainly my method of choice and the method I recommend for you! To do this most easily, you need a rotary cutter system. (See above.)

Cutting on the Lengthwise Grain
I prefer to cut strips on the lengthwise, not crosswise grain. Because most dress pattern pieces are marked "Place on the lengthwise or crosswise grain," we tend to think there is no difference. Tug on the same piece of woven fabric in both directions and you'll see that the lengthwise grain is much firmer, **Fig N**. The crosswise grain can stretch 2 1/2 to 3 times farther than the lengthwise grain. This is the main reason I stress lengthwise grain on the longest dimension of a piece whenever possible. Because all but the first two pieces in a Log Cabin block remain strips, that is they are longer than they are wide, this design is particularly sensitive to cutting strips on the lengthwise grain.

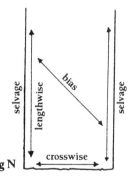

Fig N

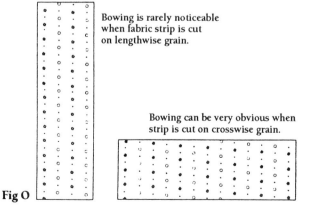

Bowing is rarely noticeable when fabric strip is cut on lengthwise grain.

Bowing can be very obvious when strip is cut on crosswise grain.

Fig O

Another important reason for cutting strips on the lengthwise grain revolves around the fabric problem called "bowing," **Fig O**. That is the word used to describe the problem of threads being pulled out of position in the printing and finishing process. Crosswise threads, instead of being perfectly perpendicular to the selvage, are arched. If you then cut crosswise strips, you are cutting (breaking) every crosswise thread you hit. Everywhere they are cut, they will ravel.

In addition, when fabric is bowed, any directional design in the fabric is pulled out of position, too. Cutting crosswise strips makes that distortion more obvious, especially in a Log Cabin strip that could be 12 to 14 inches long.

Bowing barely effects lengthwise grain. Cutting strips on the lengthwise grain keeps printed patterns more accurate and greatly reduces raveling.

Sometimes sheer economics will cause me to cut on the crosswise grain. That is, I only need a little bit of a particular fabric. When you cut lengthwise strips from a quarter yard of fabric, you can hardly call it a strip. Demands of directional fabric designs will always override grain line cutting rules.

Cutting Batting
Cutting batting with a rotary cutter does cause a bit of a problem. It seems the fibers can get caught in the little cuts that occur in mats and they are not easily removed. I have an old mat that I have designated for batting. If you don't have the luxury of a second mat, you may prefer to cut the original squares of batting with scissors. Then when it's time to trim the sewn squares, the layer of fabric between the batting and the board will protect the cutting board.

Do not cut batting and backing strips for the borders now. Wait until the quilt interior is put together and you know the exact measurements, rather than using the approximate measurements in the text.

Actual Sewing Information

Seam Allowances
The recommended seam allowance is 1/4", using 10 to 12 stitches per inch. It is not necessary to backstitch the seams as you will stitch across most ends almost immediately. If you are new to patchwork, you may not have entered the world of the 1/4" seam allowance. After using 5/8" seam allowances in dressmaking, the first 1/4" seam will look impossibly thin. Remember, many 5/8" seam allowances survive being trimmed smaller than 1/4", turned inside out and poked. The 1/4" seam allowance is adequate for patchwork, but if it is necessary to make a narrower seam allowance, don't worry until you get below 1/8".

On many sewing machines the outside edge of the presser foot is exactly 1/4" from the center of the needle hole. An easy way to measure is to put a tape measure under your presser foot, **Fig P**.

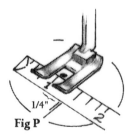

Fig P

Put any inch mark at the needle. Put the presser foot down. If it's 1/4" wide, you're lucky. If it isn't, you'll have to find some other way to calculate the 1/4" seam, like a mark on the toe of the presser foot. Tape or other marks on the sewing machine will be covered by the quilt squares.

There's More to Perfect Patchwork than a 1/4" Seam Allowance
In the final analysis, it's the size of what you see that is really important, not the size of the seam allowance. The seam allowance is there to keep the sewing threads from ripping out and to allow you to make adjustments if necessary. The object is to have a perfect 1" square, for example, in the finished patchwork, not to have a perfect 1/4" seam allowance. You can over emphasize sewing exactly 1/4" from the cut edge. It's fine when it works and if you have both a perfect finished piece and perfect seam allowance, you can feel very smug. But the most important thing is perfect size finished patchwork.

Sometimes It's Consistency that Counts
In any quilt where you are using only strips, even if they become squares, it is consistency that counts. If following the edge of your presser foot makes a seam just a **little** larger or smaller than 1/4", all that happens is that the finished block is just a **little** larger or smaller than planned – as long as all of the seams are the same.

All measurements given in this book are cut measurements. I like to use cut sizes and cut accurately. Then by sewing consistently, the finished sizes are consistent. This is not true with complicated, multi-shaped pieces and curvy lines. With those shapes, you must know exactly what size seam allowance is on the pattern and double check while sewing to be sure you are really stitching on the correct line. This is why people who love being productive, love quilts like the Weekend Log Cabin.

Pressing
Pressing is not an option. It is smart to make your iron one of your best friends, as you embark on patchwork. My preference is a steam iron. When pressing patchwork seams, both seam allowances go in the same direction, not open as in dressmaking. Usually, press them toward the darker fabric. Time spent carefully pressing is time well spent. The object is to eliminate any tiny folds I might have pressed into the seam. Tiny 1/32" folds don't seem like much until you multiply that times 2 for each seam and times 4 or 5 seams for a block and times 10 or 12 for the number of blocks. I admit to being a fanatic about perfect pressing.

Working with the Quilt-As-You-Sew method adds a new dimension to pressing that is discussed in the full instructions for the *Country Christmas Weekend Quilt*.

A Ripping Tip
If you must rip or "unsew", the gentlest way is best, especially when you have sewn through batting, backing and two fabric strips. On one side of the seam, cut around every sixth stitch. A little experimentation will let you know if you can get by with cutting every 7 or 8 stitches. Then turn the fabric over and pull the thread on the other side. When you cut at the right frequency, the thread just pops out as you pull. Go back to the first side and brush away the clipped threads.

What Size is a Quilt?

Fabric requirements are given for the quilts shown, but I'm sure you will quickly see the many possibilities available with Log Cabin quilts just by varying the size of a center square, the strips, the number of strips, etc. Then you will have to decide how big to make the strips and blocks, how many blocks to make, how many to place in each direction and what size borders to add.

When you make quilts for fun, that is, just because you want to, they can be any size. Quilts are used so many ways besides bed coverings that another view is to say that making them pretty is most important.

Size is only crucial when you are making a quilt for a specific bed or place on the wall. Then, lots of personal choices could alter the dimension. It's best to measure a specific space or bed and work with your design to get as close as possible. Remem-

ber to add 2" - 4" in each direction for the "dry shrinkage" or "take up" that occurs when quilting.

Be aware that as you get into planning quilts for specific sizes, compromises often have to be made. A 12" unit block doesn't always fit an even number of times in both directions, so that you can add an equal amount all around for borders and still come out to the exact finished size desired.

When measuring the bed isn't an option, I use these quilt size guidelines. Except for the crib size, they were developed by adding 9" for a pillow tuck at one narrow end and a 13" drop to the other three sides of standard mattress sizes.

        Crib - Small 30" x 45"; large 40" x 60"
        Twin - 65" x 97"
        Double - 80" x 97"
        Queen - 86" x 102"; Queen/Double 84" x 100"
        King - 104" x 102"

Even if you don't intend to make the Weekend Quilt, please read all of the following section.

This quilt, called the text quilt, includes all the basic construction information.
The other quilts will refer back to it and to the final section on traditional machine quilting.

MAKING THE WEEKEND QUILT

Making a Traditional Log Cabin Block

If you have never made a Log Cabin block the traditional way, I suggest you make one. It is a good way to familiarize yourself with the actual construction of the block before you start on the Quilt-As-You-Sew Weekend Quilt. Select the fabrics that you would like to use for the quilt, and follow the instructions below. The instructions here are for the block used in the *Country Christmas Weekend Quilt*, **Fig A**. It is diagonally divided into light and dark halves. Each light fabric is used twice in each half, while the dark fabrics are randomly arranged. The center square is the same width as the strips, 2 inches finished. The finished block will measure 14 inches and would make a nice pillow.

Select and prepare the fabrics for the logs and center squares and cut them into 2 1/2-inch wide strips, following the directions on page 7. Then make a block chart (see page 5) and get started. If you want to have fun making Log Cabin quilts, understanding Log Cabin block construction is critical. Even if you choose not to make this block, please read the instructions very thoroughly.

Refer to **Fig B** for the order of adding strips. Stitch the seams with a 1/4 inch seam allowance and a stitch length of 10 to 12 stitches per inch. It is not necessary to backstitch at the end of each seam as the next seam will cross over these stitches. After adding each piece, press its seam allowance away from the center square. Follow the steps 1 to 4, referring to **Fig C** on page 10.

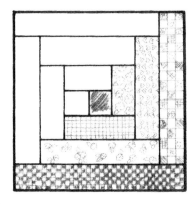

Fig A

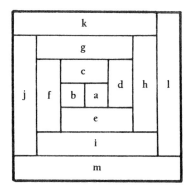

Fig B

9

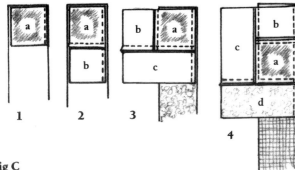

Fig C

1. Place the center square on top of the first strip of light fabric, right sides together and raw edges aligned. Seam as shown. Open and press the seam allowance away from the center square. Cut strip even with center square.

2. Turn the 2-piece unit 90° clockwise and sew again to the chosen light fabric, right sides together and one edge aligned. Press and cut.

3. Turn the 3-piece unit 90° clockwise and sew to the first strip of dark fabric, right sides together and one edge aligned. Press and cut.

4. Turn the 4-piece unit 90° clockwise and sew to the second dark fabric, right sides together and one edge aligned. Press and cut.

5. Continue to attach the appropriate strips of fabric in the clockwise order shown in **Fig B** until all twelve strips have been attached and the block is 14 1/2 inches square.

Country Christmas Weekend Quilt

APPROXIMATE SIZE: 82 X 96 inches

Armed with your newly acquired experience in constructing a Log Cabin block, you are now ready to tackle the Weekend Quilt. Do not be discouraged by the length of these instructions – you really will be able to make this quilt in a weekend. I simply believe in complete instructions and emphasize good work habits and good basic how-to techniques. You shouldn't have to figure out on your own the procedures I already know.

Do make the Weekend Quilt as your first project. It covers in detail many procedures you will be expected to know for the subsequent Log Cabin quilts and variations. Specific instructions are for the *Country Christmas Weekend Quilt* shown on the back cover. This lovely quilt is approximately 82" x 96" and fits to the dust ruffle on a queen-size bed or with a longer drop on a double. For this first quilt, do not attempt to change the size of the blocks themselves; it would be very easy to get confused. Concentrate on learning the techniques now and you will be confident in making changes in later quilts.

Materials Needed:
All yardages are approximate

Strip and Center Square Fabrics:
> 3 yds total of light fabrics
> 2 yds total of dark fabrics
> 1/4 yd center square fabric

Border and Binding Fabrics (cut crosswise and pieced):
> 1 yd for inside border
> 1 1/8 yds for middle border
> 1 1/4 yds for outside border

Backing:
> 2 1/4 yds each of two backing fabrics for squares
> 3 1/2 yds for border backing
> 3/8 yd fabric for finishing strips

Batting:
> medium weight bonded polyester

Selecting the Fabrics

As in any traditional Log Cabin Quilt, the blocks in this quilt are visually divided into light and dark halves, with a common contrasting center square. Because the strips are quite wide, the quilt is more pleasing when fabrics with less contrast are selected. High contrast from one strip to the next accentuates the width of the strips. In the text quilt, the twenty blocks can be separated into two groups of ten blocks, the blocks in each group having identical light halves. Because a large number of dark fabrics were used and the dark strips are placed randomly in the dark halves, no two blocks are alike. The light strips are identically positioned in the "L" method of arrangement, requiring six light fabrics. The two fabrics used in the **bc** position require 1/4 yard; for **fg**, 1/2 yard; and for **jk**, 5/8 yard.

The blocks are set in a pattern called Straight Furrows, said to resemble a field after plowing.

You will need to select six light fabrics (three for each of the two master blocks), one center square fabric, and at least a dozen dark fabrics ... we used twenty-two. The colors in the text quilt are not the clear pure whites, reds, and greens of a child's Christmas toy but ivory, muted greens, and Turkey reds that suggest "country." The more dark fabrics used, the less likely the creation of a double strip of fabric when the blocks are assembled into rows. The three borders repeat the Country Christmas colors.

Only two backing fabrics were chosen, one for the back of each group of ten blocks. When the blocks were assembled, these backing fabrics formed a checkerboard on the back of the quilt. See photograph of quilt back on our back cover. Contrasting finishing strips form a grid outlining the checkerboard blocks.

Cutting the Fabrics

Following the directions in "Cutting on the Lengthwise Grain" on page 7, cut your selected fabrics into 2 1/2-inch wide strips.

Cut twenty 15 1/2-inch backing squares. If you wish to duplicate the checkerboard pattern on the back of the text quilt, cut ten from one fabric and ten from a second fabric. Also cut twenty 15-inch square pieces of batting referring to "Cutting Batting" on page 8.

It is not a bad idea to cut enough fabric and batting to make twenty-two blocks (11 and 11 if you've got two basic blocks), rather than the twenty required for the quilt. Then, if a couple of the blocks are off size, they can become accompanying pillows. It does allow you to be a little more relaxed about tearing out and adjusting mistakes.

Assembling the First Master Block

Lay out strips of the center square fabric and the three light fabrics shown on your block chart and select strips of six dark fabrics. Quilt-As-You-Sew means that you seam and quilt at the same time, stitching through top fabric, batting and backing fabric as you sew each piece of your block together.

However, for the Log Cabin design, I recommend traditionally machine piecing the first five pieces, **abcde**, creating a 6 1/2-inch center unit, and then proceed with Quilt-As-You-Sew. It is much easier to accurately center and sew the large 6 1/2-inch square on the squares of batting and backing fabric, than to center the small 2 1/2-inch center square!

Because everything builds around the center block, the accuracy of it being square can not be stressed enough. In fact accuracy in every step is important.

Just a Little Strip Piecing

Pieces **a** and **b** are always the same size and in most of these quilts are the same fabric in each block. You can either cut 20 of each square and sew them together or you can cut strips of fabric as wide as the squares, sew the strips together and then cut the sewn strips into pieces as long as the square, **Fig D**. By using this Sew-Before-You-Cut technique called strip piecing, your first step is faster and more accurate than traditional piecing.

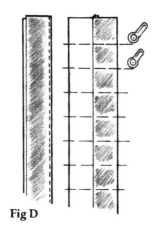

Fig D

1. Following steps two through four on page 10, continue to construct the center unit for this block by piecing strips **c**, **d** and **e** to the center square.

If you work on several identical units at a time, do not stop and break the thread and start again, but just butt the next piece up to the previous piece. This is called chain piecing, **Fig E**. Some people think chain piecing is a technique that makes the process faster. That is true, but other important benefits are consistency and accuracy. From the second unit sewn, to the last one, there is always a unit for comparison. By matching the position of the parts and watching for visual discrepancies, your blocks should be more consistent. Double check as you go! There will be several opportunities to "true up" the squares. For example, using 2 1/2 inch strips, **a** and **b** should be 2 1/2 inches by 4 1/2 inches. When **a**, **b** and **c** are combined they should be 4 1/2 inches by 4 1/2 inches square.

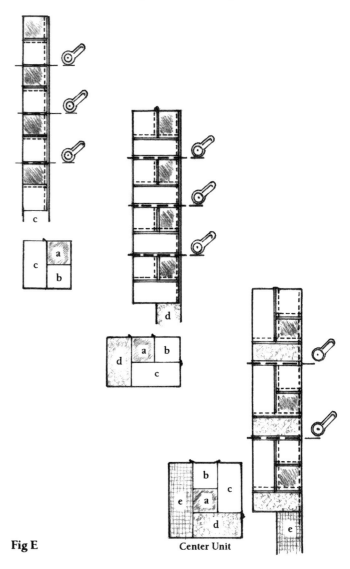

Fig E   Center Unit

2. Check the size of the center unit. It should measure 6 1/2 inches by 6 1/2 inches. Because everything builds around the center unit, the importance of it being truly square can not be stressed enough. Carefully press the square. Using a square acrylic template with printed grid lines and a rotary cutting system, trim and straighten it. If you have only a ruler, pen and scissors to do this task, consider cutting a cardboard template to look through and use for marking the cutting line.

3. Layer the batting on wrong side of backing fabric, pinning diagonally in the corners to stabilize them. Now center the previously pieced square on top of batting and pin it in place. There should be 4 1/2 inches of backing fabric on each side, **Fig F**. Quilting the center square will come after the additional strips have been added. If you chose to do it now, it would actually defeat the purpose of having the larger piece to center instead of the small square to center and sew in place.

> When you start to put the first layered square under the presser foot to get to the starting point of the seam, the presser foot and needle have a tendency to catch on the batting and you may be discouraged with the Quilt-As-You-Sew process.
>
> There is a simple solution. Turn down the corner of the batting and backing so that the smooth surface of the backing fabric covers the rough batting all the way to the edge where you will start stitching. Release the corner and smooth it back flat before starting to sew.

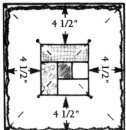

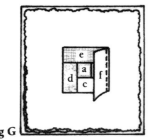

Fig F   Fig G

4. You will attach piece **f** with the Quilt-As-You-Sew method, **Fig G**. You can work either with a strip that will be trimmed later or with strips cut to length. In a recent workshop, the method of choice was about 50/50 among the participants; you will probably want to try both ways and decide for yourself. If you are using fabric scraps or if your only cutting tool is scissors, I'd advise using a longer strip and cutting it off after it is sewn. If you do so, leave a little extra fabric. Because you have to lift the strip away from the batting to cut it, you may not be as accurate as you would think. But if you have a rotary cutting system and can take advantage of its accuracy, you'll probably want to cut the strip to length before attaching it. But don't cut to length until you measure how long the strip should be. The square may have "shrunk up" in the process of being quilted, or a previous seam allowance may be a little off so that the theoretical strip length may not be the length you need!

Line up a strip of the light fabric for position **f** with the top of the center unit, right sides together and raw edges aligned. Stitch the seam through all four layers. After stitching, flip the strip away from the center unit so its right side is exposed. The seam that holds the layers together makes an indentation which holds the strip down; pressing with an iron may not be necessary. Instead, simply finger press at the corners.

Notice that when you laid down strip **f**, the edge that was not being sewn created a visible guide to be lined up parallel to a previously sewn strip. Use this same idea to help line up subsequent strips. If the distance between the unsewn edge of the strip and a previously sewn seam is equal at both the top and the bottom, the new strip is parallel. The unsewn edge of the new strip is useful in another way: when stitching the strip in place, use it as a guide for sewing straight.

5. Turn the block 90° counter clockwise and, in the same manner, stitch a strip of light fabric to the block to form piece **g**. Repeat with two dark strips for pieces **h** and **i**, Fig H.

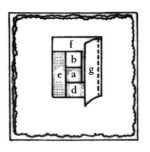
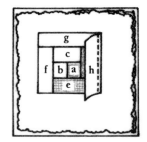

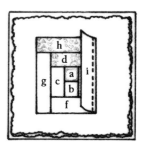

Fig H

6. Having completed the first round of strips in the Quilt-As-You-Sew method, lightly press the block to make sure the four strips are flat for the next round of stitching. Turn the block over and clip the threads off the back so they don't get tangled in the next row of stitching. Now check the dimensions of the patchwork square. It should be 10 1/2-inches square. Do you need to adjust the size by taking a smaller seam, or even changing a strip? Look for problems – and solve them – after completing each round of strips. Don't add strips to an inaccurate, out-of-shape block!

7. Proceed in the same manner to attach the final round of strips, **j**, **k**, **l** and **m**, **Fig I**. When done, the block should measure 14 1/2 inches by 14 1/2 inches.

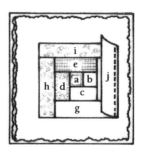
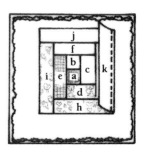

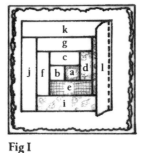
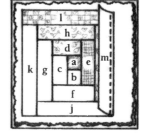
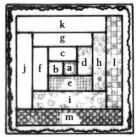

Fig I   Master Block One

12

8. Machine quilt in the ditch around the center square.

9. Make at least ten blocks following master block one.

Assembling the Second Master Block

Make a minimum of ten blocks just as you did for the first master block, but this time use the three different light fabrics shown on the block chart of your second master block.

Assembling the Quilt

1. Before doing any assembly, you'll need to trim the blocks to a consistent size. Each should be 14 1/2 inches square, but it is quite likely they will vary in size, some smaller, some larger. (The quilting itself actually takes up fabric.) So, select a size to which all of your blocks can be somehow adjusted (trimmed down, a strip replaced, a smaller seam stitched) and then adjust the blocks that need it. A different size is fine as long as all the blocks are that size. Your goal is twenty blocks of the same size. If you made extra blocks, they come in handy now ... you can set aside the most out-of-whack blocks to be used later as accessories.

There is nothing that beats a large (14" to 15") square acrylic template with printed grid lines and a rotary cutting system for trimming and squaring up the pieced blocks. If you need to do it with a ruler and pen and scissors, make sure that you make right angles at the corners. Consider cutting a cardboard window template to look through and use for marking the cutting line.

2. Lay out the blocks and decide which arrangement you like best. The arrangement shown in the photograph on the back cover, Straight Furrows, is one of my favorites for Log Cabin quilts. It is the most appropriate for Twin and King size quilts because they have an odd number of rows of blocks. Some of the other traditional Log Cabin Quilt layouts that can be made with the 20 unit blocks of the Queen/Double are Barn Raising, Pinwheel, Log Cabin Star, Zig Zag, and Pyramid. See page 14. In the diagrams, the dark L represents the corner where the dark side of the block is positioned. I usually try to avoid double strips of high contrast fabrics, formed when the outermost logs in two adjacent blocks are cut from the same fabric.

> **WHAT IF YOU HAD MORE BLOCKS?**
> If the quilt had 24 blocks instead of 20, several of the designs shown would be symmetrical and look more complete. The quilt would be 82" x 110". You might want to try it on your next quilt. But before you rush into that, think about this. Flat on paper, 20 blocks looks quite incomplete. However, if you place the 20 blocks on a bed, so that the 16 blocks that have a complete or symmetrical design are between the pillows and the foot of the bed, it looks pretty good. The quilt is flat under decorative pillows and the four odd blocks are covered by the pillows, so you really don't notice that the design seems incomplete. Just take a look at *Kittens in the Garden* on the front cover.

If you have an instant camera (or are willing to wait for 1 hour processing), it is fun to arrange the blocks several different ways, photograph them, and then compare the photos of the arrangements before deciding for sure which way to assemble the blocks. It seems that each set of fabrics selected looks better in some arrangements than others.

If you used several contrasting fabrics for the backing squares, remember to check the arrangement on the back of the quilt also. After you decide which arrangement you prefer, it is a good idea to label the blocks with pieces of masking tape, identifying their positions, before picking them up again.

3. Assemble the horizontal rows first. Perhaps you've been wondering how we are going to sew the blocks together without having a lot of raw edges showing on the back. You're right, it can't just be a simple seam. There must be a way to cover that. At one time I used to work hard to disguise the block method. It was quite laborious. It was the part people didn't like. Now, assembling with an added covering or finishing strip is my favorite way of finishing the blocks' raw edges. Sometimes I even use the strips to be decorative on the back.

The finishing strips are cut on the lengthwise grain 1 1/2 inches wide and about 1 1/2 inches longer than the lengths of the blocks or rows of blocks to be joined. For the text quilt, cut fifteen strips 1 1/2 inches wide by 16 inches long. Press the strips in half lengthwise, wrong sides together. Then layer two adjacent blocks, right sides together and place a folded strip on the blocks, aligning all raw edges. Pin in place and stitch 1/4 inch from the raw edges through all eight layers, **Fig J**.

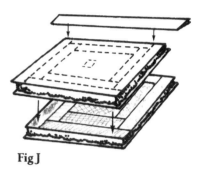

Fig J

A friend discovered that if you pull the block firmly over your knee, the seam opens up and it is easy to trim away the excess batting in the seam allowance between the layers of fabric. It is not necessary to cut away fabric, except at the ends of the blocks where the next seam will be. After trimming the batting, press the strip to the side so that it covers the raw edges and hand stitch it in place with a hidden stitch.

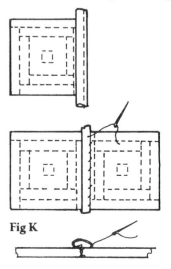

The finishing strip is always pressed toward (and hand stitched to) the block it did not touch when sewn, **Fig K**. If you have chosen a fabric for the finishing strip that contrasts with one or both of the backing squares, it is important to decide on which square you wish the strip to lie and to take care to pin it to the appropriate block before stitching.

Fig K

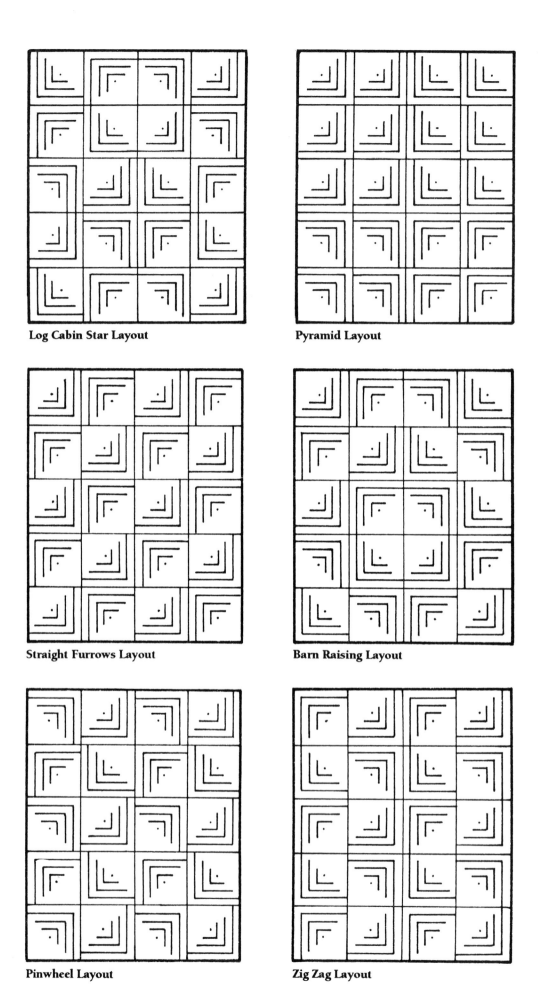

Log Cabin Star Layout

Pyramid Layout

Straight Furrows Layout

Barn Raising Layout

Pinwheel Layout

Zig Zag Layout

Alternating strip direction, **Fig L**, in adjacent horizontal rows reduces bulk at the seam intersection when the rows are joined, while not alternating strips allows you to develop a grid system that lines up and creates a nice secondary pattern on the back of your quilt.

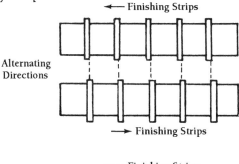

Alternating Directions

← Finishing Strips

→ Finishing Strips

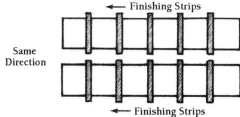

Same Direction

← Finishing Strips

← Finishing Strips

Fig L

4. Join the five horizontal rows with four finishing strips, each 1 1/2 inches wide by 58 inches long. (Piece as necessary to get the length.) Proceed as above, considering to which side you wish the finishing strip to be hand stitched before pinning it to the rows of blocks to be joined.

Other Finishing Options
Serging
What about serging these seams? Personally, I'm quite a proponent of the serger and feel we should use it more, but I feel that serged seams in this area are not quite adequate for a bed quilt. They could be considered for a wall hanging. If you do serge the seams, you will probably want to reverse them at intersections because of the bulk.

Machine Hemming
If you are clever with your sewing machine and know how to use your machine hemming feature, it is possible to hem the finishing strips and eliminate the hand stitching.

Eliminating Some Finishing Strips
When the **m** strip is on the vertical edge where two blocks are being sewn, it is possible to join the blocks by stitching only 5 layers, leaving one block back unattached, then turning it under 1/4" and stitching in place by hand. This method eliminates bulk and a couple of steps on those particular blocks, but does mean your technique is not consistent throughout. It is especially suitable when all the backing fabric and strips match.

Adding Borders Quilt-as-You-Sew
Adding the First Border
If the quilt will be finished with a separate binding, the batting and border backing pieces are cut to extend about 1 inch beyond the last border. If the quilt will be finished with a self-finished edge, the batting is cut to extend about 1 inch beyond

the last border but the backing should extend 1 1/2 inches beyond the last border.

1. Cut four each of the border, batting, and border backing pieces needed for your quilt. Because the batting and border backing strips cover the total width of the three front borders, they are cut much wider than any of the border strips.

Cut the border strips on the lengthwise grain, if possible. Do not cut your borders until you have measured your own quilt and found the exact lengths you will need.

2. Add the side borders first. Lay the quilt on a large flat surface right side up and put one of the side border pieces on top, right side down with one long edge lined up with the long edge of the quilt. Pin in place sparingly. To add the batting and border backing fabric, fold the pinned edge of the quilt back about 15 inches, **Fig M**. Place the backing fabric strip against the backing of the quilt, right sides together. Put the batting on top of it. Line up raw edges and ends, **Fig N**, then pin securely in place through all six layers. Machine stitch 1/4 inch from the raw edges, through all six layers, the entire length of the quilt. Remove pins.

3. Repeat step two on the opposite long edge of the quilt, **Fig O**.

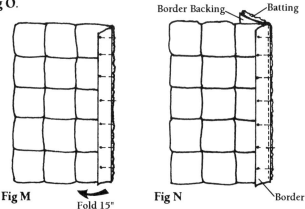

Border Backing

Batting

Fig M

Fold 15"

Fig N

Border

4. Trim away any excess batting from the seams to reduce bulk, but do not trim closer than 1/8" or batting will tend to pull out of the seam. Pull the front border, batting, and border backing away from the quilt and bring them together so they are flat on the same surface as the quilt, as on the right edge of **Fig O**. The batting is now sandwiched between the border and the border backing fabric. This is the one seam that I recommend pressing – preferably with steam.

5. Position the end pieces of the first border, border backing, and batting as shown in **Fig P**. The two strips of end border

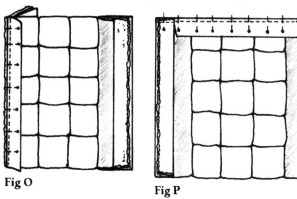

Fig O

Fig P

fabric do not go the full width of the quilt, as the batting and border backing do, but end even with the outer edges of the side border strips. Trim the border ends to exact length as necessary. Pin securely, machine stitch, trim the excess batting, and pull the borders forward as in steps two through five. Press the seam. Repeat on the other end.

Adding Subsequent Borders

Now that the batting and border backings are in place, adding subsequent borders is quick and easy.

1. Pin the first borders flat. Along one long edge, place a strip of the second border fabric on top of first border, right sides facing and raw edges matching and pin them securely. The ends of the second border should line up with the ends of the first border, **Fig Q**.

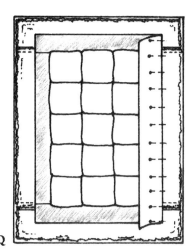

Fig Q

2. Machine stitch through both borders, batting and backing fabric 1/4 inch from the raw edges of the borders. Align and stitch the second long edge in the same manner. After removing the pins, pull the second border forward to lie flat on the batting. Press.

3. Add the second border at both short ends of the quilt. The end strips go from one end of the second side border to the other, **Fig R**.

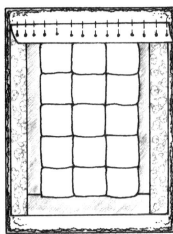

Fig R

BINDING THE QUILTS
Self-binding

To self-bind a quilt, the border backing fabric pieces (for Quilt-As-You-Sew borders) or quilt backing fabrics (for non-Quilt-As-You-Sew borders) are cut large enough to be wrapped to the front of the quilt and bind the raw edge. This is another way of minimizing the time required to finish a quilt. The measurements for border backings allowed in the text quilt did allow for this finish.

After adding the borders, there should be an even amount (about 1/2 inch) of batting left around the outside edges of the quilt and an even greater amount (about 1 1/2 inch) of backing fabric left around the edges of the batting, **Fig S**. To hem the quilt, fold the excess backing fabric about 1/2 inch then fold it again over the edge of the batting and border, **Fig T**. Pin in place. Hand-hem or machine topstitch near the folded edge to finish the quilt. If hand stitching, make sure the stitches catch completely through the backing fabric to secure the batting in place. If machine stitching, consider using the invisible thread and your machine hemming stitch.

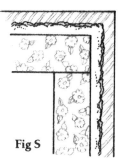

Fig S

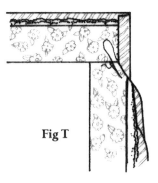

Fig T

It's Not Done Until It's Signed

We often urge that quilts be signed and dated so that future quilt historians will know who made them. Log Cabin Weekend Quilts are made to be used, not preserved, but that is an even more important reason to sign them. Forget about the historians, sign and date the quilts you make for the people you know and love who are using them. Signing can be as simple or elaborate as you desire. It can go on the front or the back.

A really simple way, is to use an indelible marking pen or laundry pen to write your name, date and any inscription on a piece of pre-washed muslin or other fabric. Then hand stitch this to the back of the quilt.

16

OTHER LOG CABIN QUILTS MADE QUILT-AS-YOU-SEW

The three quilts in this section are also made Quilt-As-You-Sew. The first, *Kittens in the Garden*, is a variation of the *Country Christmas Weekend Quilt* – the two master blocks for *Kittens in the Garden* are the same size as those for *Country Christmas* and have an equal number of the same size strips. Only the fabrics, the positioning of the fabrics in the master blocks, and the set of the blocks has been changed.

The *12 Block Log Cabin Crib Quilt* is made with the same number of strips per block, but they are 1/2" narrower.

The *Star Set Log Cabin* is elegantly simple and shows a very unique use of fabric. One large print was cut for all of the strips on the dark half of the block.

The last quilt in this section, *Pinwheel Log Cabin Quilt* is also very different. Faced with its forty-eight small blocks each with twenty thin strips, you are unlikely to make the *Pinwheel Log Cabin Quilt* in a weekend unless you are team quilting. But Quilt-As-You-Sew is still a wonderful technique to use for it ... imagine the time spent otherwise!

Kittens in the Garden

APPROXIMATE SIZE: 84 X 96 inches

Kittens in the Garden was made in the same way as the *Country Christmas Weekend Quilt*, but with different fabrics in the two master blocks.

The blocks are set in a Barn Raising arrangement. When it came time to lay the blocks out, I resisted my colleagues' suggestion to even try this arrangement, knowing that "double strips" would appear ... a problem I try to avoid. Fortunately, they insisted. Yes, the quilt does have double strips, but I find that I don't mind. In fact, I even like them and the "maze" effect that they give! I credit this surprising result to the medium weight of the colors in the double strips – a floral with hidden kitties. In addition, the constant position of the dark blue makes a nice center square and the sea foam green strips add a sparkling accent.

I still say, if we had exchanged the positions of the master blocks in the quilt, the resulting high contrast navy double strips of second master block would be very distracting and detract from the look of the quilt! This group of blocks did not look nearly as pretty when arranged in the Straight Furrows arrangement. That is why it is worth the effort to look at several different arrangements.

The blocks and borders were made just like the *Country Christmas Weekend Quilt*. The individual border widths vary just a little because we liked the effect better. The quilt is finished with a separate binding.

Kittens in the Garden

Materials Needed:
** All yardages approximate **

Four light fabrics:
>   3/8 yd of a light fabric (strips bc - blocks 1 and 2)
>   3/4 yd of a light fabric (strips fg - blocks 1 and 2)
>   5/8 yd of a light fabric (jk - block 1)
>   5/8 yd of a light fabric (jk - block 2)

Five dark fabrics:
>   1/2 yd of a dark fabric (de - blocks 1 and 2)
>   1/2 yd of a dark fabric (hi - block 1)
>   1/2 yd of a dark fabric (hi - block 2)
>   3/4 yd of a dark fabric (lm - block 1)
>   3/4 yd of a dark fabric (lm - block 2)

Center fabrics and inside border:
>   1/4 yd of center square fabric
>   1 yd of inside border fabric*

Outer borders:
>   1 1/8 yd middle border fabric*
>   1 1/2 yd outside border fabric*

Backing fabrics:
>   8 yds for backing of squares, borders, and finishing strips
>   3/4 yd for separate binding

Batting:
>   med weight bonded polyester - twenty 15" squares

*cut crosswise and pieced

Selecting the Fabrics

In the *Country Christmas Weekend Quilt*, the blocks within a master group are not identical: they have matching light halves but different dark halves. In *Kittens in the Garden*, however, the ten blocks in each of the two master groups are identical. In other words, there are ten exact copies of master block 1 and of master block 2. Additionally, the central unit **abcde**, is the same for all twenty blocks.

Each fabric is used twice in a block, making a pair of logs which form an "L" shape. Since there are six "L's" in each of the two master blocks, you would think you would need twelve log fabrics for the quilt. We, however, repeated two of the light fabrics and one of the dark fabrics in both master blocks, cutting the total number of log fabrics for the quilt to ten. The kitty floral fabric is a real attention-getter; it sets the mood for the quilt. The light fabrics pick up the pink and blue of the kitty fabric as do two of the other dark fabrics. A dark navy floral and a green small print add some necessary contrast. The center squares are a deep pink. The backing fabric matches throughout.

Cutting the Fabric

Cut the log fabrics and center square fabric into 2 1/2-inch wide strips. Also cut twenty 15 1/2-inch squares each of backing fabric and twenty 15-inch squares of batting.

Assembling the Block

Assemble twenty matching **abcde** central units and then ten each of both block 1 and block 2 following the general directions for the *Country Christmas Weekend Quilt* but using the fabric selected. See pages 9 to 13.

Assembling and Finishing the Quilt

Following steps one through four on pages 13 to 15, assemble the quilt. The block arrangement for *Kittens in the Garden* is shown in **Fig A**. To finish the quilt, refer to pages 15 and 16. We attached three borders (3 1/2, 4 1/2, and 5 1/2 inches) Quilt-As-You-Sew and cut a separate binding. Feel free to design your own borders. The fabrics you choose for your quilt may look best with different numbers or sizes of borders.

Fig A

12 Block Log Cabin Crib Quilt

APPROXIMATE SIZE: 41 1/2 x 51 1/2 inches

This charming crib quilt has the same basic block as the *Country Christmas Weekend Quilt*, the strips are just cut 1/2 inch narrower, **Fig B**. Only 12 blocks are made and it is set in the Straight Furrows setting. The same sweet juvenile print is used in all the strips on the light side of the block and the random placed assorted blue, pink, sea foam and yellow prints complete the dark side, proving that the fabrics are only dark relative to the light side.

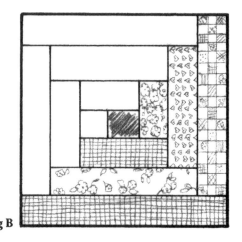

Fig B

The borders (1, 1 3/4, and 3 inches) are added Quilt-As-You-Sew, with a separate 1/4-inch finished binding.

18

Materials Needed:
All yardages are approximate

Strip and Center Square Fabrics:
> 3/4 yd assorted prints
> > (16 in photographed quilt)
> 3/4 yd of a light print
> 1/8 yd for center squares

Border and Binding Fabrics (cut crosswise and pieced):
> 1/4 yd for inner border
> 3/8 yd for middle border
> 5/8 yd for outer border
> 3/8 yd for binding

Backing:
> 1 3/8 yds for backing squares
> 1 yd for border backing (cut crosswise)
> 3/8 yd for finishing strips

Batting:
> medium weight bonded polyester

Selecting the Fabrics
Your local fabric store most likely will have a number of juvenile prints that will be well-suited to making a crib quilt. Whether choosing lights or brights, be sure your fabric colors harmonize.

Cutting the Fabric
Cut the light and dark fabrics into 2-inch wide strips. Cut twelve 2-inch center squares. Cut twelve 12-inch squares of backing fabric and twelve 11 1/2-inch squares of batting.

Assembling the Block
Assemble the twelve blocks following the general directions for the *Country Christmas Weekend Quilt*, pages 10 to 13, but using the fabrics selected.

Assembling and Finishing the Quilt
Trim the blocks to a consistent size. Following steps one through four on pages 13 to 15, and looking at the diagram of the Straight Furrows setting on page 14, assemble the quilt. To finish the quilt, we added three borders Quilt-As-You-Sew, and cut a separate binding. We machine quilted in the ditch around the strips and borders. As always, feel free to design your own borders. You may prefer different numbers or sizes of borders for your quilt.

Star Set Log Cabin Wall Hanging
APPROXIMATE SIZE: 52 x 52 inches

If you are a closet quilting fan, avidly wanting to make a beautiful quilt but sidelined by a dread of selecting and coordinating scores of fabrics, take heart ... a Log Cabin quilt need not contain dozens of fabrics to be interesting, nor must the fabrics be traditional "quilter's prints." This elegant wall hanging uses only three fabrics and is especially interesting because both the dark logs and the border come from a single 54-inch wide home decorating fabric. Two floral stripes, 9 1/2-inches wide and 4-inches wide, ran the length of the taupe, burgundy, and mauve chintz that was chosen. All dark logs

were cut from the wide 9 1/2 inch stripes and the narrow 4- inch stripes were saved for the outside border. The sixteen blocks are identical (there is one master block), **Fig C**, and are set four by four, **Fig D**, so that their dark halves form a large star, a pattern called "Ohio Star." A narrow 3/4-inch finished inner mauve border and a 1/2 inch mauve binding set off the 3 1/2 inch floral border.

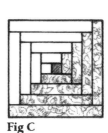

Fig C

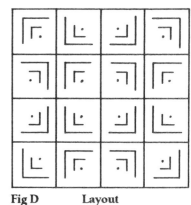

Fig D　　**Layout**

Materials Needed:
All yardages are approximate

Center Square, Border and Binding Fabric (cut crosswise and pieced):
> 1 yd mauve for inner border, binding, and center squares

Floral Stripe Home Decorating Fabric (54" wide)
> 1 1/2 yds for floral border and "dark" strips - cut lengthwise

Light Fabric (or muslin):
> 1 yd for light strips
> 3/8 yd for finishing strips

Backing:
> 3 1/8 yds for backing squares and border backing

Batting:
> medium weight bonded polyester

Selecting the Fabrics

The home decorating section of your local fabric store most likely displays dozens of lovely drapery and upholstery fabrics. If you go to a specialty home decorating fabric shop, expect to find hundreds of these gorgeous fabrics. We used a floral stripe from which both the logs and the second border could be cut, but don't limit yourself to this type of fabric. Groups of coordinating home decorating fabrics are widely available; you could cut your strips from one fabric and your border from another. Large florals are fine, although you probably will want to make sure that each strip can be cut entirely from the floral, with no "blank" patches of background fabric. Decorator fabrics are often 100% cotton, but with a finish to inhibit soiling, labeled "dry clean," which would make the care of the quilt different from most. The backing squares are cut from plain muslin.

Cutting the Fabric

Cut the light and dark fabrics into 1 3/4-inch wide strips. Cut sixteen 1 3/4-inch center squares. Cut sixteen 13 1/2-inch squares of backing fabric and sixteen 13-inch squares of batting.

Assembling the Block

The wall hanging contains sixteen identical blocks. For each block, machine-piece the first round of strips (**b** through **e**) to the center square and then continue Quilt-As-You-Sew, beginning with strip f. Since the five-piece center units are all the same, you can chain-piece them to save time and increase accuracy. The center units should be 4 1/4 inches square and the completed sixteen strip blocks 11 3/4 inches square. Quilt around the center squares when the blocks are complete.

Assembling and Finishing the Quilt

Trim and straighten the blocks, lay them out, and then join them with finishing strips, following steps three and four on pages 13 to 15. For the "Ohio Star" pattern, you will need twelve strips (approximately 1 1/2 inches wide by 13 1/2 inches long) to assemble the blocks into rows, and three strips (approximately 1 1/2 inches wide by 48 inches long) to join the rows. Remember to cut the finishing strips to the length correct for your quilt, approximately 1 1/2 inches longer than the blocks or rows of blocks that they are to join. The 3/4-inch inner border (cut 1 1/4 inches) and the 3 1/2 inches (cut 4 inches) floral border were added Quilt-As-You-Sew, with mitered corners. A separate binding hems the quilt.

Refer to Finishing the Quilt, pages 41 to 44, to add borders, batting, and border backing and bindings for your quilt.

Pinwheel Log Cabin Quilt

APPROXIMATE SIZE: 82 x 102 inches

This earth-tone quilt is one of my favorite quilts. It was constructed with forty-eight different 11-inch square log cabin blocks, each with twenty thin (1-inch finished) strips, **Fig E**. The blocks feature the same deep rust center square and are divided

Fig E

diagonally into traditional light and dark halves. Because the center square is the same width as the strips which form the logs, the dark and light halves of the block are divided by a visually pleasing "perfect stair step."

The blocks are set six by eight in a pinwheel pattern which makes a wonderful diagonal illusion. In this quilt, the backing square fabrics were chosen and the blocks arranged to also form a patchwork pattern on the back; see photograph on page 25.

Materials Needed:
All yardages are approximate

Strip and Center Square fabrics:
 3 1/2 yds assorted light fabrics
 4 yds assorted dark fabrics
 1/8 yd for center squares

Border and Binding fabrics (cut crosswise and pieced):
 5/8 yd fabric for inner border
 1/2 yd each of three fabrics for middle borders
 1 3/4 yds fabric for outside border
 3/4 yd fabric for binding

Backing:
 8 yds (can be assorted fabrics)
Batting:
 medium weight bonded polyester

(continued on page 25)

▲ **Pinwheel Log Cabin Quilt - page 20**

◄ **Pineapple Block Pillow - page 26**

21

Little Blue Quilt - page 29

Crazy Log Cabin - page 34   Star Set Log Cabin Wall Hanging - page 19

12 Block Log Cabin
Crib Quilt - page 18

How Much Is That Doggie
in the Window? - page 30

Shaded Chevrons - page 34

23

▲ Linked Chevrons - page 36
   Papa Bear (left)
   Mama Bear (on wall)
   Baby Bear (right)

▶ Full Spectrum - page 32

24

(continued from page 20)

Back of Pinwheel Quilt

Fig F   **Pinwheel Quilt Layout**

Selecting the Fabrics

Approximately 26 dark fabrics and 10 light fabrics were used for the strips for the forty-eight blocks. The colors were chosen from a limited palette: subdued brown, green, rust, and burgundy "darks"; tan and ecru "lights." In this block, each fabric is used twice, making a pair of "logs" which form an "L" shape. Choose five light and five dark fabrics for each block in addition to the center square fabric. Random use of scraps within the dark and light parameters allows you to include as much or as little of a particular fabric as you want, or have.

Cutting the Fabrics

Cut your selected fabrics into 1 1/2-inch wide strips. Cut forty-eight 12-inch backing squares from these same fabrics. If you wish to duplicate the checkerboard pattern on the back of the photographed quilt, cut twenty-four squares from light fabrics and twenty-four from dark fabrics. Also cut forty-eight 11 1/2-inch square pieces of batting.

Assembling the Block

Select strips of the center square fabric, five light fabrics and five dark fabrics. Cut center square strips into 1 1/2-inch squares.

Construct the center unit for this block by machine-piecing strips **b** through **e** to the center square. The center unit should measure 3 1/2 inches by 3 1/2 inches. Press, trim and straighten the unit before proceeding Quilt-As-You-Sew for four complete rounds. Remember to check the block dimensions frequently, adjusting the strips and your seams as necessary to keep the block square. When finished, the block should measure 11 1/2 inches square.

Assembling and Finishing the Quilt

Once again the first step is to trim the blocks to a consistent size. Each should theoretically be 11 1/2 inches square but a different size is fine as long as all forty-eight blocks are the same size. In fact, each strip in the blocks on the quilt pictured is slightly narrower than calculated so that the blocks were only 11 inches. We just made slightly larger borders than originally planned. To duplicate the photographed quilt, lay out the blocks as in **Fig F** so the dark halves of the blocks form pinwheels. If you used several contrasting fabrics for the backing squares, check the arrangement on the back of the quilt also. Label the blocks with pieces of masking tape, identifying their positions, before picking them up again.

Assemble the blocks into rows following the directions on pages 13 to 15. Use forty finishing strips 1 1/2 inches wide and approximately 13 inches long. Join the eight rows with strips about 70 inches long. Finally, add the borders and hem the quilt referring to pages 40 through 44. The five Quilt-As-You-Sew borders for the *Pinwheel Log Cabin Quilt* are finished widths of 2 1/4 inches, 1 inch, 1 inch, 1 inch, and 5 1/2 inches. The three 1-inch borders have mitered corners. The quilt was bound separately. As always, your fabric choice could change the arrangement or number or proportion of borders needed to complete your quilt most pleasingly.

25

A LOG CABIN VARIATION MADE QUILT-AS-YOU-SEW

At first glance, one might think that the pineapple block, shown in **Fig A**, is pieced from triangles – not just one triangle but dozens of differently sized triangles! But actually, the Pineapple design is a Log Cabin variation and is constructed "Log Cabin style" with strips of fabric in concentric rings around a center square. The Pineapple block differs, however, because its strips are not all parallel to the center square; alternate strips lie diagonally. The Pineapple takes longer to make than the Log Cabin because there are twice as many strips in each round of construction, eight instead of four.

Fig A

The center square in the Pineapple block is most often dark and the strips surrounding it alternate light and dark. The resulting Pineapple block has dark diagonal "arms" and light horizontal and vertical "arms." As in the Log Cabin block, you can create an astonishing variety of looks by varying the fabrics, "log" width, center square size, and the set of the blocks.

Pineapple Block

APPROXIMATE SIZE: 15 X 15 inches

As for the *Country Christmas Weekend Quilt,* our first Pineapple project will be a single block, without batting and backing fabric, that can be made into a pillow like our photographed pillow on page 21. For the block shown in **Fig A**, five rounds of 1 3/4-inch strips – alternating light and dark – were stitched to a 3-inch center square. The corners were finished with two additional dark strips.

Materials Needed:

Scraps totaling approximately 1/2 yard:
    1/4 yd assorted light fabric
    1/4 yd assorted dark fabric

Selecting the Fabrics

Twenty light fabrics and twenty-nine dark fabrics were used in this block. The light fabrics had similar ecru backgrounds. Green, blue, and red dark fabrics were selected.

Cutting the Fabrics

Cut one 3-inch center square. Cut the remaining fabric into 1 3/4-inch wide strips.

Assembling the Block

The strips are sewn to the center square in the order shown in **Fig B**. The first two strips in each round are stitched to opposite sides of the block as are each subsequent pair of strips in the round. It is not necessary to backstitch at the end of each seam as the next seam will cross over these stitches. After adding each strip, flip it open to expose its right side and press its seam allowance away from the center square.

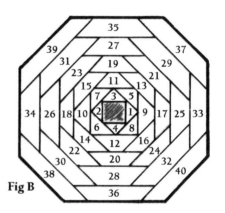

Fig B

1. Stitch the first two strips of light fabric, one and two, to opposite sides of the center square, right sides together and raw edges aligned. The ends of the strips will be trimmed later; simply be sure the strip is at least 3 inches long before stitching, **Fig C**.

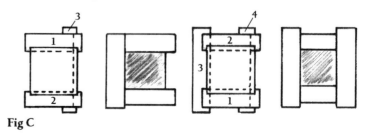

Fig C

26

2. Stitch the remaining two strips of light fabric in the first round, three and four, to the center square. Stitch approximately 1/2 inch beyond the center square on both sides, joining these strips to the first two light strips as well as to the center square.

3. Draw a 4-inch square diagonally on the pieced block, as shown in **Fig D**. Be accurate – the raw edges of the next strips will be lined up on these lines! The points of the center square should be 1/4-inch inside the drawn square. To double check your drawn square, draw two diagonal lines through the center square, **Fig E**. They should make four perfect 2-inch squares inside the 4-inch square.

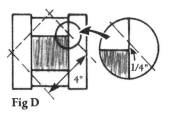

Fig D

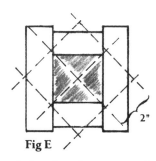

Fig E

A clear acrylic 4-inch square with ruled grid markings is terrific for marking the square. If you don't have one, make a cardboard template with a 4-inch square window.

4. Line up the raw edges of the first two dark strips, five and six, on two opposing sides of the 4-inch drawn square. Remember to keep right sides together, **Fig F**; stitch. Flip strip over to right side and cut the ends of the dark strips parallel to, and slightly longer than, the outer edges of the light strips they cover.

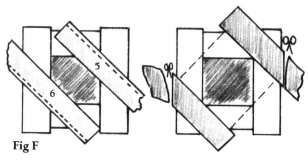

Fig F

5. Attach the remaining two dark strips, seven and eight, in a similar manner. The first round is complete. Now, flip and cut the ends of all the dark strips as shown in **Fig G**. The newly cut edges of the block will be parallel to the sides of the center square and 1/4 inch outside the points of the "light" square. Now is a good time to turn the block over and trim the trim the threads to keep them from getting caught in the next stitching.

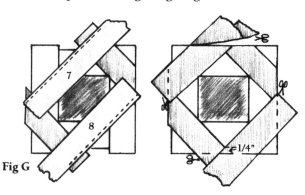

Fig G

6. Begin the second round by stitching two strips of light fabric, nine and ten, to opposing long sides of the block, right sides together and raw edges aligned. Use the edge of the center square as a guide to keep the strips straight. Repeat with strips eleven and twelve. As shown in **Fig H**, trim the ends of the light strips even with the outer edges of the 1 1/2-inch wide dark strips. The newly cut edges of the block will be parallel to the sides of the "light" square and 1 1/2 inches outside it.

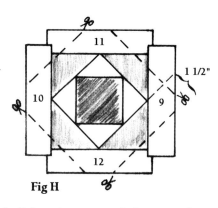

Fig H

7. Finish the second round and continue in the same manner until all five rounds have been attached and the block is approximately 14 1/2 inches square. Remember you can use previously sewn seams as guides for keeping the strips straight as you attach them.

8. After completing the fifth and final round, finish the corners. To duplicate the photographed block, add two more dark strips to each corner and trim the ends of these strips even with the long sides of the block. The last strip will extend only slightly beyond the seam allowance intersection, **Fig I**.

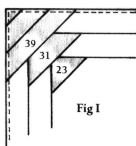

Fig I

You may finish your corners differently, **Fig J**. Try inserting a narrow contrasting strip in the corner before adding the last two strips or using a triangle instead of strips, perhaps even a pieced triangle.

9. Handle the block very gently or staystitch the edges so that its many bias edges do not stretch and pucker. Assemble projects that use Pineapple blocks quickly, soon after the blocks are finished.

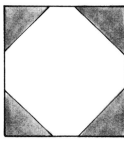

Fig J   Corner Finishes

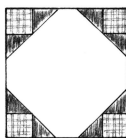

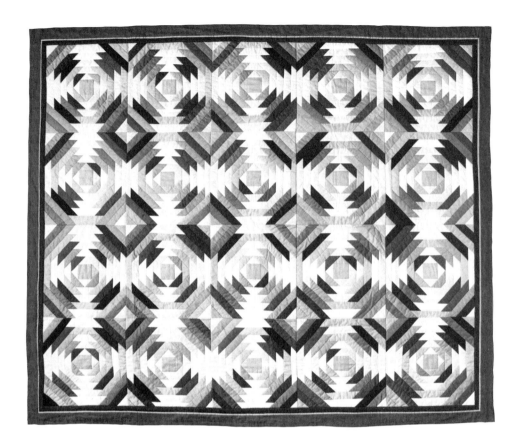

Springmaid® Celebration Quilt

APPROXIMATE SIZE: 65 x 78 inches

Materials Needed:
All yardages are approximate

Strip and Center Square Fabric:
> 1/4 yd fabric for center squares
> 2 3/8 yds assorted light fabrics for strips
> 3 1/2 yds assorted bright fabrics for strips

Border Fabrics (cut crosswise and pieced):
> 3/8 yd for inner border
> 1/4 yd for middle border
> 3/4 yd for outer border

Backing Fabrics:
> 1/2 yd for finishing strips
> 4 1/2 yds for backing squares and border backing

Batting:
> medium weight bonded polyester

Selecting the Fabrics

This quilt was made in the 100th anniversary year of Springs Industries. The challenge was to incorporate all of the 100% solid color cotton fabrics in the Springmaid® Natural Charm line into one quilt, so the selection was done for me. Developing the balance of the colors and deciding on an appropriate pattern was next. I decided to treat it like a scrap quilt and divided the colors into light and dark. The darks were further sub-divided into areas where certain colors were used randomly. For example, most of the light, bright colors that were classified as dark were used in the first two rounds of construction.

For even more fun, the squares for the back of this quilt were pieced from Springmaid® cotton prints in the line the same year.

Cutting the Fabrics

The center squares are cut 3 inches by 3 inches. The strips are cut 1 3/4 inches wide **except** the last row on the straight sides. Cutting the last row of strips 2 inches wide prevents any skimpy seam problems. However, it is easy to confuse 2-inch and 1 3/4-inch strips, so either don't cut any 2-inch strips until you get to the last round, or keep them carefully isolated. Cut twenty 16 1/2-inch squares of batting and twenty 17-inch squares of backing fabric.

The borders are 1, 3/4 and 2 inches. You might easily prefer another arrangement.

Assembling the Block

1. Pre-piece the center square and the first four strips. They are the first four light strips. They only need to be as long as the square. Draw the four-inch square diagonally in the center as you did for the single Pineapple Block on page 27.

2. Layer batting and backing as for the *Country Christmas Weekend Quilt* and center pre-pieced unit right side up on batting.

3. Proceed as for the individual block, except on the last round of strips on the straight sides, substitute the 2-inch wide strips.

Assembling the Quilt

When blocks are complete, trim to common size and join blocks as in other Quilt-As-You-Sew quilts. Add borders and finish as desired.

Log Cabin Quilts Not Made Quilt-As-You-Sew

Little Blue Quilt

APPROXIMATE SIZE: 35 1/2 x 35 1/2 inches

This is the first quilt to be discussed that is not made Quilt-As-You-Sew. Quilts with small blocks have just too many seams to finish the backs using finishing strips. *Little Blue Quilt* is a fairly intricate scrap quilt with sixteen small (6-inch) blocks set four by four. As a wall hanging it could be made Quilt-As-You-Sew, but as a full-size quilt it would require way too many finishing strips!

Note the color and position of the center squares in this quilt. Traditionally, center squares are dark (often red) and lie squarely in the center of the blocks. Here, however, they are muslin and offset! Why is that? Well, we used a "trick." You can subtly emphasize one half of a Log Cabin block by attaching more logs on that side. The colors or tones of the fabrics in the "larger" half of the block will then predominate because these fabrics actually cover more of the block. In this quilt, the light half of each block has four logs, two on each side, and the dark half has six. We cleverly disguise this technique (and keep the block from looking lopsided) by making the center square the same tone as the half with fewer logs, in this case the light one. When the center square is visually part of the "smaller" half of the block, a "perfect stair step" divides the block diagonally and hides the disparate sizes of the two halves.

The borders of *Little Blue Quilt* are particularly striking and are more complex than those in the previous quilts. The 1 3/4-inches (finished) wide inner blue border is highlighted by a single white square in each corner. The outer 4-inch wide (finished) mitered border is pieced from 1-inch strips of the same fabrics used in the blocks. *Little Blue Quilt* was machine quilted in the ditch around the blocks and borders. This is a very adequate finish for a wall hanging, but add more quilting if you are going to use this as a crib quilt.

Materials Needed:
All yardages are approximate

Strip, Center Square, and Pieced Border Fabrics:
       1/2 yd assorted light prints for strips
          (8 in photographed quilt)
       1 yd assorted dark prints for strips
          (16 in photographed quilt)
       1/4 yd muslin for center squares and strips
       Note: If strips are cut crosswise, 1/8 yd of each fabric
         is needed.

Inner Border and Binding Fabrics (cut crosswise and pieced):
       3/8 yd blue print for inner border
       1/4 yd muslin for binding and border squares

Backing:
       1 1/8 yds

Batting:
       medium weight bonded polyester

Selecting the Fabrics

Each log in one of these ten-log blocks is cut from a different fabric. So, to reproduce the *Little Blue Quilt*, you will need four light fabrics and six dark fabrics per block. This does not mean you must have sixty-four (16 x 4) light fabrics and ninety-six (16 x 6) dark fabrics, but do use a lot! *Little Blue* was made from 25 fabrics – ivories, rosy reds, plums and (of course) blues. I find scrap quilts most delightful when they include a great variety of fabrics. Reuse fabrics in different blocks but vary their positions. To camouflage the lopsided block and create a perfect stair step, select a light fabric for the center square; ours is muslin. The backing fabric was a solid piece of blue print.

Cutting the Fabrics

Cut the scraps into 1 1/2-inch strips, both for the Log Cabin blocks and for the pieced outer border. Cut sixteen 1 1/2-inch center squares.

Assembling the Block

Machine-piece ten logs around a center square for each block, referring to **Fig A** for the order of construction. Check the size of the blocks as you go and adjust as necessary. When complete, the blocks should measure 6 1/2 inches square.

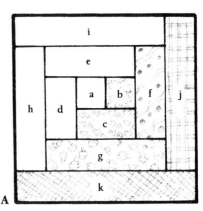

Fig A

Fig B

Little Blue Quilt Layout

Assembling the Quilt Top

Trim the blocks to a consistent size and then lay them out. Avoid placing the blocks so that "double strips" result. For the arrangement in **Fig B**, that means not setting two blocks together if they use the same fabric for dark logs **j** and **k**. You may label the blocks with pieces of masking tape to identify their position; but, if you use the "pairs" method of assembling the blocks into a quilt top (described below), that is not really necessary. With the blocks laid out on the floor in the arrangement you like...

1. Flip the second column of blocks face down on the first and pick up the resulting pairs of blocks, working from the bottom of the quilt to the top and placing each subsequent pair of blocks on the top of your stack. The pair of blocks from the upper left corner of the quilt ends up on the top of the stack. Carefully take the stack to the sewing machine, keeping the "hinged" side of the pairs of blocks on the right. Chain piece, starting with the pair on the top of the stack. Make sure you are seaming the edge that was between columns one and two. Lay the new column of blocks (1 and 2) back down. Do not cut the threads – the chain piecing automatically keeps them in the right order.

2. Repeat with columns three and four.

3. Press the seam allowances of the pairs of blocks to one side, pressing in the same direction for all pairs of blocks across a horizontal row and alternating direction (left, right, left, right) for each pair in a column. As you press, a little ridge develops on the front side of the block. If you press properly, when you position these pairs together for the next seam, the ridges will just meet and will act like little grippers. No basting, no pinning! Always think ahead and press for "automatic pinning."

4. Now sew pairs of pairs. Flip the top pair of blocks in newly created column 1 and 2 face down on the pair below it. Stitch and press. In the same manner, join the third and fourth sets of pairs in column 1 and 2. Repeat with the pairs in column 3 and 4. You will generate four-block units without having to match more than one seam. Don't cut the threads keeping the columns in line yet; they are still keeping order.

5. Now sew pairs of pairs of pairs. Flip the top four-block unit in column 1 and 2 face down on the four-block unit below it. Stitch and press. Repeat for column 3 and 4. Once again you have only had to match a single seam.

6. Finish by joining the two eight-block units.

Finishing the Quilt

Complete instructions for finishing the quilt are found on pages 40 to 44. You will need to cut backing fabric and batting; layer, pin, and machine quilt the quilt top, batting, and backing fabric; add border with corner blocks and mitered pieced border; and bind the quilt edges. The borders were added traditionally. The quilt was bound with a 3/8-inch separate binding.

To make the pieced outer border, stitch 1 1/2 inch-wide scraps together until you have four strips of fabric as long as you need. Start with scraps somewhat longer than the cut width of the border, then use a rotary cutter and straight edge to trim the pieced strips to width. Use these strips as the fabric for the outer mitered border.

How Much Is That Doggie in the Window?

APPROXIMATE SIZE: 47 x 47 inches

One day when I was cleaning, I found this darling doggie applique left over from a machine applique project. That started me thinking, and this charming quilt with the applique as a focal point is the result. Why the name? Well, look at the block in **Fig C**. This is not a Log Cabin block but another traditional block called Puss in the Window. Now look at the photograph of *How Much Is That Doggie in the Window?* on page 31. You can see that the quilt looks just like a gigantic single block of Puss in the Window – the diagonal halves of the Log Cabin blocks taking the place of the triangles in Puss in the Window. The thirty-two Log Cabin blocks in this quilt form a "frame" around a "window," in which sits, not a cat, but the doggie applique.

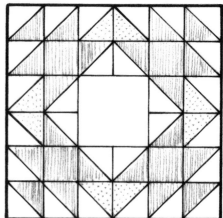

Fig C

Puss in the Window Block

We have included a scaled-down drawing of the doggie for those quilters who wish to reproduce this quilt exactly. But don't feel you must use it! Any other applique would do. This would also be a terrific spot for one of the lovely pre-printed fabric panels on the market or even a picture you have fabric painted yourself!

This quilt will make you reexamine your definitions of "light" and "dark" fabrics. Just as "Puss in the Window" requires triangles of very light, light, medium, and dark fabrics, this quilt needs Log Cabin blocks with very light, light, medium, and dark halves, **Fig D**. These four differently toned halves are combined to make the four types of blocks shown in **Fig E**. ("A"-very light/light, "B"-light/medium, "C"-light/dark, "D"-medium/dark). Each block still has a lighter and darker half, but the fabrics themselves are not necessarily "light" and "dark."

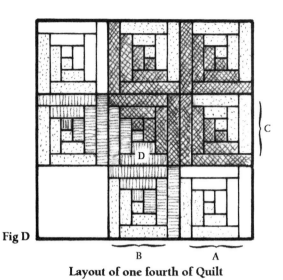

Fig D

Layout of one fourth of Quilt

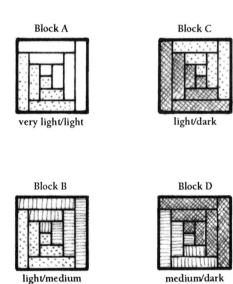

Fig E

As did the blocks in the *Little Blue Quilt*, the blocks in this quilt have fewer logs in one half. The resulting offset center square is not apparent because it matches the tone of the half of the block with fewer logs, making a perfect stair step.

The photographed quilt has three borders, 1 1/2 inch, 1 1/2 inch, and 3 inches wide, and is hemmed by a separate 1/2-inch binding. The quilt top was pinned to the batting and backing fabric and then machine quilted. The borders were added in a modified Quilt-As-You-Sew method. The quilt interior was centered on batting and backing as large as the finished quilt would need. Then the borders were added as the second and subsequent borders on the Quilt-As-You-Sew method.

Materials Needed:
All yardages are approximate

Strip and Center Square Fabrics:
     1/4 yd peach plaid
     3/8 yd muslin
     1/4 yd each of at least six different light prints
     1/4 yd each of at least eight different dark prints

Applique:
     1/4 yd brown print
     1/8 yd brown print
     1/8 yd dk green solid
     3/8 yd pink solid

Borders and Binding Fabrics (cut crosswise and pieced):
     1/4 yd rose print for inner border
     1/4 yd small brown print for middle border
     5/8 yd large brown print for outer border
     5/8 yd peach plaid for binding

Backing:
     3 yds

Batting:
     medium weight bonded polyester

Selecting the Fabrics

Select several fabrics in four different tone groups for the logs –very light, light, medium dark, and dark. In the photographed quilt, the very light fabric was a muslin, lights were peachy-pink prints with white or ivory backgrounds, and the medium and dark fabrics were peach-pinks, cinnamons, and browns. The center squares of blocks "B," "C," and "D" match the lighter side of their blocks; those of block "A" match the darker side.

We picked up the color of the center applique in the three borders. You may get tired of hearing this, but you should design your quilt borders to enhance your own quilt, not mine. The fabrics you choose for your quilt may need borders of different width, number, or proportion to set them off the best. For the photographed quilt, we used a small peach print for the backing fabric and a deep brown print for the border backing pieces.

Cutting the Fabrics
Cut the log fabrics into 1 1/2-inch wide strips. Cut thirty-two center squares 1 1/2 inches wide by 1 1/2 inches high. The center panel for the applique is cut 12 1/2 inches square.

Assembling the Block
Make eight blocks "A," eight blocks "B," twelve blocks "C," and four blocks "D" (see **Fig E**). For each block, machine-piece ten strips around a center square. Blocks should be 6 1/2 inches square when finished.

Scale-up the reduced drawing of the doggie in **Fig F** and applique it to the center panel or prepare your own center panel.

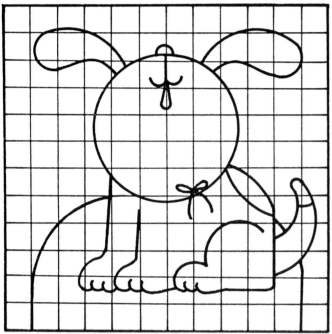

Fig F   Each square to be enlarged to 1" for doggie applique

Assembling and Finishing the Quilt
Trim the blocks to a consistent size, lay them out as in photograph, then assemble the quilt top. Use the "pairs" method described on page 30 to sew the blocks and center panel together. Layer the quilt top, batting, and backing fabric, pin securely, and machine quilt around the blocks, following the directions on page 41. The three borders were attached Quilt-As-You-Sew, see page 15. You may want to duplicate the border quantities and widths or design your own. *How Much Is That Doggie in the Window?* was hemmed with a separate binding.

Full Spectrum
APPROXIMATE SIZE: 52 x 52 inches

This striking contemporary wall hanging is constructed from thirty-six 6-inch blocks, nine each of four basic blocks. The well-defined dark halves are identical: their center squares and logs are black. The light halves of the blocks are themselves divided diagonally into quarters of two harmonious colors. This is an excellent example of how varying log width can influence the look of a block. You will notice that the black strips are cut narrower than the colored strips. That is not immediately noticeable in the finished wall hanging but that is how the curved effect was created. In addition, the colored areas of the quilt predominate; narrower black strips mean less black overall in the wall hanging. Also, by making the center square black, the block had four strips of color on each side and only three strips of black, decreasing again the amount of black in the surface of the quilt.

The machine-pieced blocks are set six by six and surrounded by several borders, three plain black borders and two pieced spectrum borders, one simple and one more complex. It is finished with a separate black binding.

Materials Needed:
All yardages are approximate

Strip and Pieced Border Fabrics:
    1 1/8 yd black for strips
    1/2 yd each of eight different prints (hand-dyed)

Borders and Binding Fabrics (cut crosswise and pieced):
    1 1/8 yd black for inside, middle and outer borders
    5/8 yd black for binding

Backing:
    3 yds

Batting:
    medium weight bonded polyester

Selecting the Fabrics
Nine fabrics were used in this wall hanging: a rich black and eight intense hand-dyed colors. Four pairs of harmonious colors are used in the light halves of the four basic blocks; pink and purple, blue and blue-green, green and yellow, red and orange. (Harmonious colors are those that merge into each other in a rainbow and are adjacent to each other on a color wheel.) When the blocks are assembled into the the wall hanging, the full spectrum appears, an entire color wheel.

Cutting the Fabrics
Cut the black fabric into 1 1/8-inch strips and thirty-six 1 1/2-inch squares. Cut the colored fabrics into 1 1/2-inch strips.

Assembling the Block
Assemble each block following the block chart in **Fig G**. Because you will be making more than one of each block, chain piecing

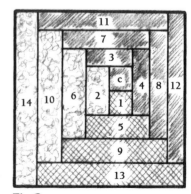

Fig G

32

and completing one color combination before starting the next would be an easy way to keep order. Check the dimensions of the blocks frequently and adjust as necessary. A completed block with fourteen strips should be 6 1/2 inches square.

Assembling and Finishing the Quilt

Trim, lay out and assemble the blocks as described in text quilt on page 30. Assemble the blocks into sets of four first, **Fig H**, then join them into rows, and join the rows.

The quilt top and borders were pieced traditionally and machine quilted in the ditch. The middle tie-dyed border has mitered corners. See pages 40 to 41 for instructions.

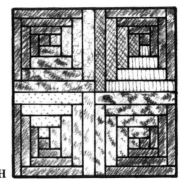

Fig H

LOG CABIN VARIATIONS NOT MADE QUILT-AS-YOU-SEW

Crazy Log Cabin

APPROXIMATE SIZE: 27 x 35 inches

This grouping of hand-dyed fabrics was perfect for playing with the *Crazy Log Cabin*, or the quilt affectionately called "For People Who Can't Cut Even Strips." It was quilted by machine in the ditch after being assembled.

Materials Needed:
All yardages are approximate

Strip, Center Square, Triangle, and Block Fabrics:
> 1/4 yd each of nine assorted fabrics for strips
> 1/4 yd dark fabric for solid blocks
> 5/8 yd light fabric for center squares, floating triangles, and corner triangles
> Border and Binding Fabrics (cut crosswise and pieced):
> 3/8 yd dark fabric for border
> 1/8 yd med fabric for corner border squares (or use scraps from strips)
> 3/8 yd floral print for binding

Backing:
> 1 1/8 yds

Batting:
> medium weight bonded polyester

Selecting the Fabrics
The hand-dyed fabrics used were purchased in a set. If selecting fabrics individually, look for a pleasant blending similar to this.

Cutting the Fabrics
Instead of cutting even strips, these strips are cut quite haphazardly in a thin to wide strip.

Assembling the Block
The assembly of the block starts from the center and spirals just like the original Log Cabin, **Fig A**. Reversing whether you are starting with the thin or wide end keeps some semblance of square. You still may have to occasionally add a strip out of sequence. Try to keep the centers somewhere near the center.

It is a good idea to practice a few squares to get the hang of being so inaccurate!

Assembling the Quilt
The blocks are set diagonally—see *Linked Chevron* for "Assembling the Quilt", page 38. The quilt was bound with a print that picked up the color story.

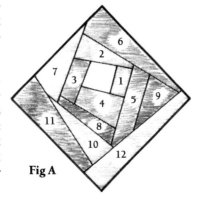

Fig A

Crazy Log Cabin

Shaded Chevrons

APPROXIMATE SIZE: 32 x 32 inches

The basic block of the Chevron Log Cabin starts with one small square, just like the Log Cabin, but instead of building on all four sides, strips are added alternately on two sides. Almost always the same fabric is used for two consecutive strips to create the Chevron, **Fig B**. It is then most frequently put together in a diagonal set. That means the individual blocks appear to be balanced on a corner instead of resting flat on one side.

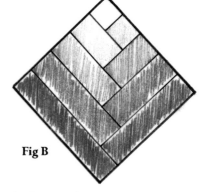

Fig B

Diagonal sets look great, but they do create a new challenge around the outside edge of the quilt as empty triangular spaces are created. In this *Shaded Chevrons* quilt, those spaces were filled with solid pieces of fabric as the color gradation was such an important part of the visual impact of the quilt. (See Step 4 on page 39). In other quilts you might decide to continue the Chevron design. You would make more pieced blocks and cut them in half. When you make the seam on the outside edge, the half blocks aren't quite big enough on the outside edge. The seam will nip off a tiny corner of the full blocks. If that puts you in a panic, the only option is to design new half blocks with larger strips and piece them appropriately.

Shaded Chevrons

Materials Needed:
All yardages are approximate

Triangle, Strip, Border and Binding Fabrics:
      1/4 yd fabric a (lightest)
      3/8 yd fabric b
      3/8 yd fabric c
      1/2 yd fabric d
      3/8 yd fabric e
      3/8 yd fabric f
      1/4 yd fabric g
      1/4 yd fabric h (darkest)
      3/4 yd fabric for outer border (tie-dyed)

Backing Fabric:
      1 1/8 yds

Batting:
      medium weight bonded polyester

Selecting the Fabrics
The fabrics used in this quilt are hand-dyed in equal gradation from light to dark and beige to plum. The Chevron is especially effective when fabrics selected are progressive.

Cutting the Fabrics
Strips are cut 1 1/4 inches wide. See "Cutting the Fabrics" for the *Linked Chevron* quilts on page 38.

Assembling the Block
If using solid colors, make block as described in introductory paragraph. If using prints, you may want to read ahead to "Assembling the Blocks" and use the Sew-Before-You-Cut Two-Strip method, page 38.

Assembling the Quilt
Using the diagonal set (page 38), assemble blocks as shown in the photographed quilt or as you desire. We alternated pieced blocks with solid blocks. Note that we used two colors for the inside border and binding to accent the shading variations, and we used a tie-dyed outside border that incorporated all the shades and colors used in the quilt. Be creative to add interest to your quilt.

Batting and backing were layered with the quilt top, and the interior of the quilt was machine quilted in the ditch. Then borders were added using the modified Quilt-As-You-Sew method. A 1/2-inch separate binding was used to finish the quilt. See page 43 for details.

Mama & Baby Linked Chevron Layout

Linked Chevrons

Often it is the interplay between blocks that makes a quilt exciting. With just a little extra thought, but no extra work, the *Linked Chevron* is a perfect example. By carefully selecting your fabrics, the darkest strips will make a fascinating all-over design. And the next darkest, will make a secondary linked design.

Study the layout for *Mama and Baby Bear* and you will see that there are only two master unit blocks. Each block is a Chevron Log Cabin with all strips of equal width and only four fabrics per block. You will also observe that the order of the fabrics simply reverses in the second block.

There are two small quilts shown and one that was made for a 3/4-size water bed. Except for the width of the strips, they were all made using the layout. The larger *Papa Bear* quilt had 18 more blocks added for extra length.

When using strip techniques and pattern free patchwork, you are able to decide what size you want the finished piece to be by deciding what size your starting strip will be. The starting strips for the three quilts are only 1/4 inch different (Baby Bear, 1 1/2" strips, Mama Bear, 1 3/4" strips, and Papa Bear, 2" strips), yet each quilt is about 9" wider and 11" longer for each 1/4 inch extra in the strips. It is a very vivid example of how much variation in size you can get with such a little change in the size of the strip.

The smaller quilts are very quick and good to make if you just want to try the techniques. There is also a layout on page 39 for a full-size quilt that requires 110 blocks starting with a 2-inch cut strip.

Baby Bear Linked Chevron

Mama Bear Linked Chevron

Papa Bear Linked Chevron

Baby Bear
APPROXIMATE SIZE: 42 x 52 inches

Materials Needed:
All yardages are approximate

Strip and Center squares:
    3/8 yd each of cream, camel,
      blue, and plum prints

Triangles:
    1/2 yd camel print

Borders and Binding (cut crosswise
and pieced):
    1/4 yd camel print for inner
      border
    1/4 yd cream print for middle
      border
    1 yd blue print for outer border
    1/2 yd cream print for binding
    1/4 yd muslin for flap border

Backing fabric:
    1 5/8 yds

Batting:
    medium weight bonded polyester

Mama Bear
APPROXIMATE SIZE: 49 x 62 inches

Materials Needed:
All yardages are approximate

Strips and Center Squares:
    1/2 yd each of cream, camel, dk
      green and dk red prints

Triangles:
    1/2 yd camel print

Borders and Bindings (cut crosswise
and pieced):
    3/8 yd dk green floral print for
      inner border
    1/4 yd dk red print for middle
      flap border
    1 1/4 yds dk green for outer
      border
    5/8 yds camel print for binding

Backing:
    3 yds

Batting:
    medium weight bonded polyester

Papa Bear
APPROXIMATE SIZE: 62 x 94 inches

Materials Needed:
All yardages are approximate

Strips and Center Squares:
    3/4 yd each of med teal, dk teal,
      rust, and rose prints

Triangles:
    1 3/8 yds med teal print

Borders and Binding (cut crosswise
and pieced):
    3/8 yd lt teal print for inner
      border
    1/2 yd rust print for middle
      border
    1 7/8 yds dk teal for outer border
    3/4 yd dk teal for binding

Backing:
    5 1/4 yds

Batting:
    medium weight bonded polyester

Selecting the Fabrics

The most important thing is to have light, medium and dark fabrics to develop two linked chevrons. The dark one is usually the dominant and the light one the secondary. When the strips are wider, I like to use lower contrast fabrics to de-emphasize the larger strips. In other words, large strips in high contrast colors can look real klunky!

I prefer to select a fabric similar to, but not matching one of the medium strips for the setting triangles. If you use one of the fabrics in the strip sets for the setting triangles, the strips look like they are emptying or flowing out of the quilt and into the edge.

Cutting the Fabrics

Because so many of these strips are sewn together in their entirety, think about placing the fabrics that will be sewn together right sides together before cutting. Then the strips are in the right position for the first seam.

Assembling the Blocks

The blocks could be made one strip at a time, but there is another Sew-Before-You-Cut trick that can be applied to this block, especially when you are using prints. In the One-Strip Chevron, the fabrics make the "L" shape, as the same fabric is used on both sides of the square and the direction of the seams alternates, **Fig C**.

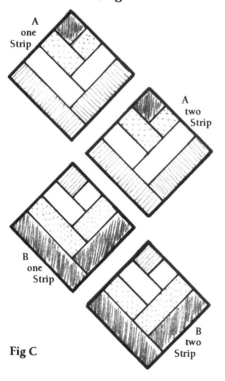

Fig C

Look at the Two-Strip Chevron made with the fabric in the same position. The "L" shape looks the same, the only difference is the arrangement of the seam lines and three less steps on each of at least 67 blocks. That eliminates a lot of start and stop sewing!

Granted, the long strips still have to be sewn together, but that doesn't begin to equal the work eliminated. If you are using solid colors, the seam lines might be too visible and distracting to use the Two-Strip Method.

Making Block A Using the Two-Strip Method

Assemble the necessary number of Block A as follows:

1. Piece strips together as shown in **Fig D**. Press toward the dominant fabric.

2. Cut the 1 & 2 strip for your block in increments equal to the cut width of your strips, **Fig E**.

3. Chain piece the cut 1 & 2 pieces onto the fabric 2 side of the 2 & 3 strip as shown, **Fig F**. Press, cut apart using the 1 & 2 piece as your measure.

4. Chain piece the new 1 & 2, 2 & 3 section onto the 3 & 4 strip set, **Fig G**.

5. Complete the Chevron by piecing the new 6-strip unit to the single strip, **Fig H**.

Making Block B

Reverse the order of fabrics and make the necessary number of B blocks.

Assembling the Quilt

At this point, you may lay all blocks out individually and assemble by rows or you can continue chain piecing some of the blocks together, making pairs of A and B blocks and then pairs of pairs. It must be done with the blocks in the right relationship to create the overall pattern eventually. Check and double check. The layout for a full-size quilt shows the progression from pairs, to pairs of pairs, to rows, to a quilt.

1. Stack all the B blocks face up with the dominant fabric square in the lower right hand corner.

2. Place an A block face down on a block B with the dominant "L" in the lower right hand corner. Stitch the right edges together so that when

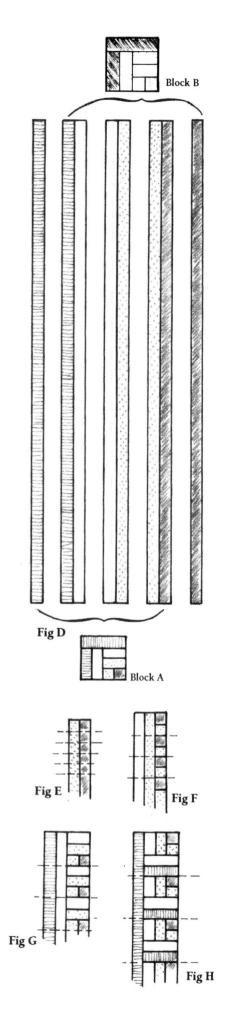

Block B

Fig D

Block A

Fig E

Fig F

Fig G

Fig H

opened the pairs look like **Fig I**. Study the diagram of the quilt you are making to count how many blocks should not be sewn into pairs. It is just a few per quilt.

3. Diagonal set quilts really are easier to piece in diagonal rows because the setting triangles need to be added at the end of most rows. However, this quilt can have one more pair of blocks chain pieced and still be easy to work with.

With one of the pairs you have just pieced face up as shown, **Fig I**, lay another pair face down with opposite dominant shapes touching. Chain piece the right hand side.

4. Cut appropriate setting triangles using the following method. To make setting triangles with the hypotenuse or long side on the straight grain, we make a larger square and cut it in quarters diagonally, **Fig J**. What size is the square you plan to quarter? Measure the diagonal of the unit block and add 1 1/4 inches. That is the length of the side of the square you will quarter for a perfect, no mistakes fit, **Fig K**. I prefer to make the setting blocks larger so that the design blocks float inside the borders instead of being crushed by them. For the starting square size for cutting setting triangles that float, add 1 1/2 to 2 1/2 inches to the length of the diagonal of the unit block.

The four corner triangles can be cut from two squares the same size as the unit block, **Fig L**. They will be oversized enough to match large floating setting triangles. The excess can be trimmed away later.

Lay the quilt blocks out on the floor and fill in edges with single block and setting triangles as shown in quilt layout. Stitch setting triangles and single unit blocks into place and complete rows.

5. Batting and backing fabric were cut and layered for the full size of the quilt, then the quilt top interior section was centered on them and machine quilted in the ditch. Then borders were added using the modified Quilt-As-You-Sew method. A 1/2-inch separate binding was used to finish each quilt. See "Finishing the Quilt" section for details on modified Quilt-As-You-Sew borders and bindings.

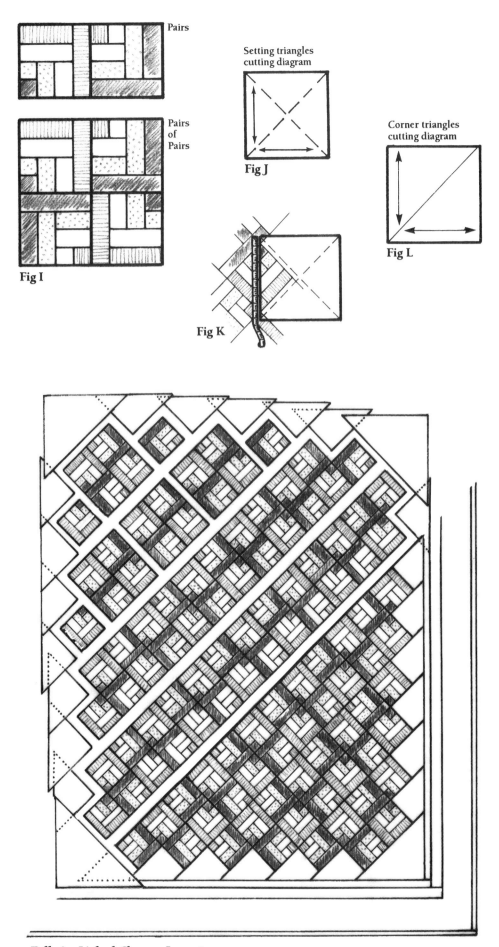

Full-size Linked Chevron Layout

39

FINISHING THE QUILT

Finishing Your Quilt Top

If you haven't chosen to use the Quilt-As-You-Sew method or have made one of the quilts with smaller blocks where it is not as appropriate, you may need some information on adding borders, traditional machine quilting, separate bindings and other finishing touches.

The methods I use most are machine quilting "in the ditch", modified Quilt-As-You-Sew borders and finishing with a separate French fold binding, cut on the straight grain.

In Book One of this series, "Quilting for People Who Don't Have Time to Quilt" (ASN 4111), we introduced straight line machine quilting "in the ditch" and the modified Quilt-As-You-Sew method for adding borders. Book Two, "Strip, Trip and Shadow Quilts for People Who Don't Have Time to Quilt" (ASN 4120), reviewed those techniques and included an introduction to free form machine quilting and machine quilting large quilts in sections. This book has emphasized complete Quilt-As-You-Sew techniques so it will include only a limited review of the machine quilting. For more information please refer to these previous books.

Adding Borders

If you thought all your choices were over when the Log Cabin blocks were made, think again! The first step in adding borders to your quilt is really designing them. That is, picking the number of borders, their widths and the fabrics. It is important that you feel free to design your own borders. The fabrics and set of each group of Log Cabin blocks strongly affect a quilt's look. The borders and binding that complement the strong country colors of the *Country Christmas Weekend Quilt* may not flatter your own pastel print version. I design my borders not only to arrive at a certain finished quilt size, but also to make the quilt more attractive.

You also have the choice of when to add borders. They can be added to the quilt top only, or during the Modified Quilt-As-You-Sew or Quilt-As-You-Sew processes. These instructions are for quilt top only, but most of this information is used in all methods. The variations are given later in this chapter.

Before doing any work with borders, it is important to measure your quilt carefully and accurately. If the measurements on opposite borders do not match, this is your first opportunity to make corrections. If you don't correct it now, the error just gets more exaggerated with each border.

Adding Blunt Borders

1. Determine the desired width of the first border. Add 1/2 inch for seam allowances. Cut two side borders that width and the exact length of the quilt.

The length of the top and bottom borders is the width of the quilt top plus twice the desired finished border width plus 1/2 inch for seam allowances. Cut two.

> Some people add extra length to their borders, "just in case". It is true that it is easy to cut excess fabric from a border and impossible to stretch it. However, if that "just in case" extra length gets unintentionally eased into the border, you are actually creating a ruffle. Granted, it has very little fullness, but it is fuller on the outside edge than on the seam edge and will never lay really flat again.
>
> So, I say, cut your borders the exact length they should be and make sure your quilt fits it. Mark and match the center point and quarter points of both the quilt and the border.

2. Add both side borders first. Lay the quilt top on a large flat surface, right side up, and put one of the side border pieces on top, right side down and one long edge aligned with one long edge of the quilt. Pin in place and stitch 1/4 inch from the raw edge, **Fig A**.

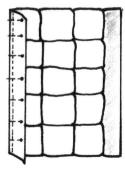

Fig A

3. Pull the borders away from the quilt top and press. Make sure the new corners are square and the opposite sides are equal lengths.

4. Add the top and bottom borders in the same manner.

5. Repeat steps one through four for subsequent borders. Always attach the side borders first and complete one set of borders before starting the next.

Adding a Blunt Border with Corner Blocks

1. Determine the desired width of the first border. Add 1/2 inch for seam allowances. Cut two side borders that width and the length of the quilt. Add as above.

2. Cut 4 contrasting squares the same size as the border is wide.

3. Cut the top and bottom borders 1/2 inch longer than the width of the quilt before borders. Add one square to each end of the top and bottom border strips. Matching seams carefully, add borders as above.

Adding a Mitered Border

There are only a few mitered corners in the whole book, and even they were really mock mitered. There are several reasons for this. Mitered corners take more time, more fabric, more skill and lots more luck than blunt corners. When the same non-directional fabric is being used in the entire border, the resulting corners look the same whether they are blunt seamed or mitered, **Fig B**. In addition, I have a Theory.

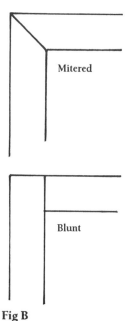

Mitered

Blunt

Fig B

40

THE MITERED CORNER QUOTA THEORY

I believe that we are all born with an unknown quota for the number of perfect mitered corners we can make in a lifetime. I would hate to be 85 years old and have a great floral striped border fabric that just had to be mitered and discover that I had used up my quota mitering something as undemanding as muslin. So I save my mitering for corners where it really counts.

There is a corollary to this theory that says, "Only three out of four mitered corners can be perfect on the same quilt on the first try!"

Borders that will be mitered have to be cut longer than blunt finish borders. When cutting mitered borders, the length of the top and bottom borders is calculated by adding the width of the quilt **plus** the width of **two** finished borders **plus** 1/2 inch. That is the way to calculate the length of all borders with mitered corners. They must be positioned perfectly and sewn to the side of the quilt stopping 1/4 inch from the end of the quilt. Press seam allowance toward quilt top.

To stitch the miter, the quilt is folded at a 45 degree angle with the borders perfectly aligned on top of each other. Continue the fold line with the stitching, **Fig C**.

For a mock miter, work from the top of the quilt with one border extended flat and the other folded and pressed to make the perfect 45 degree angle. Pin in place and carefully stitch by hand with a hidden stitch, **Fig D**.

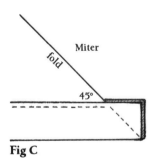

Fig C

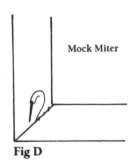

Fig D

When corners are completed to satisfaction, trim away the excess fabric and proceed. It is okay to miter one border and not the others. I used both methods in the *Pinwheel Log Cabin* and the *Full Spectrum*.

Preparing the Backing Fabric

Before cutting any batting or backing fabric, you must decide whether to add the borders Quilt-As-You-Sew or traditionally and whether to hem the quilt with a separate binding or a self-finished edge. The batting and backing fabric are cut to different sizes for the different finishing techniques.

Full Quilt Top

When adding a separate binding, I cut backings about two inches bigger in all directions than the quilt top and even that is more for convenience than necessity. (If you want to bind the edges by bringing the backing around to the front, the backing size needs to be 2 1/2 to 3 1/2 inches larger.)

On small crib or wall quilts it's usually not necessary to piece backings. The typical 45-inch wide fabric is wide enough and you just cut it slightly longer than the quilt.

Usually a quilt back is made from one fabric with minimal piecing. Nothing says that has to be. In fact, I find more and more of my quilt backs incorporating some degree of patchwork, a trick that allows me to use up fabric from my reserves so I can buy new fabric for tops!

The most common pieced back is a single seam centered lengthwise. Sometimes it is advantageous to make crosswise seams. See **Fig E**.

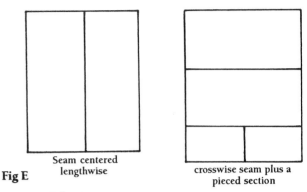

Seam centered
lengthwise

Fig E

crosswise seam plus a
pieced section

Batting Selection

For minimal machine quilting, my favorite batting is the same bonded polyester, medium weight batting I use for Quilt-As-You-Sew. When I am planning on doing a dense machine quilting pattern, I select a lighter batting. See page 6 for more discussion on batting.

Preparing Quilt Tops for Quilting
Layering and Pin-basting the Quilt Top

1. When backing, batting and quilt top are all prepared, layer them very carefully with backing right side down on a smooth hard surface, the batting smoothed and centered on top of the backing and the quilt top pressed and positioned right side up on the batting. Packaged batting should be removed from its bag a day or two ahead of time so it can relax. A careful steam press eliminates humps and bumps.

2. Pin all layers together with rust resistant safety pins, or hand baste. Straight pins are not an alternative because they catch on the quilt and can scratch you badly as you are working. Work from the center out. Every time you move the quilt, double check to make sure you haven't developed wrinkles or folds in the backing fabric.

3. If you are not familiar with this process, see either of the first two books in this series. This is a suitable method for either hand or machine quilting, but our emphasis is on machine quilting.

Machine Quilting the Quilt Top

Nearly everyone wonders if they need a fancy machine to do the quilting. I have successfully machine quilted with all kinds of machines from very simple to the most expensive. Check your machine's quilting I.Q. on scraps first. If you have any problem, or don't like the look of the stitch, the first thing to check is the pressure of the presser foot. Too much pressure can make an undesirable rippling effect. Nearly every machine has an even feed attachment available that helps move all layers through the machine at the same rate. One machine even has a built-in even feed, which, I must admit, is my favorite for machine quilting "in the ditch".

MACHINE QUILTING "in the ditch"

"In the ditch" refers to stitching in the space created between two pieces of fabric that are sewn together. "What space?", you say. Granted there isn't much, so you create a little more space by applying slight tension. Your fingers won't just walk, they'll pull away from the seam as the sewing machine feed dog pulls the fabric through the machine. That slight tension creates the extra space for stitching. When your fingers release the tension, the fabric returns to its natural position and tends to hide the stitching "in the ditch".

Setting Up the Machine

For most of the "in the ditch" quilting, I like to use invisible nylon thread for the top thread only. In the bobbin use a cotton or cotton wrapped polyester thread that matches the color of the backing fabric. The invisible thread comes in both smoky and clear. I use smoky for everything but the lightest fabrics. The clear seems to reflect light and show more than the smoky. If I will be stitching on or beside only one color, I prefer to use the 100% cotton thread on the top also.

It is usually necessary to loosen the tension for the nylon thread. It is very stretchy and if the tension is too tight, the thread stretches while sewn and draws up and puckers when you stop sewing. I like a stitch length of 8 to 10 stitches per inch for quilting.

Folding the Quilt

The trickiest part of machine quilting is fitting an enormous bulky quilt under the comparatively tiny arch of a sewing machine. The only way to handle this is to make the quilt smaller and more manageable. The lengthwise center seam will be the first place to quilt. Before sewing, I roll the right side of the quilt to within four to five inches of the center seam. Fold the left side in nine to ten inch folds to within the same distance from the seam, **Fig F**. Then, roll the quilt up like a sleeping bag, starting at the end opposite from where you want to start sewing, **Fig G**. Now you are in control.

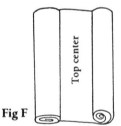

Fig F   Fig G

The Actual Quilting

1. Roll the quilt and place the exposed end of the lengthwise center seam under the sewing machine foot. Pull the quilt away from the seam with both hands to make a "ditch." Position a friend or table in front of the sewing machine to catch the quilt as you sew; if it is not supported, the weight of the sewn quilt will pull too much on the unsewn part of the quilt.

2. Reroll the quilt and stitch the center horizontal seam. Stitch the remaining seams. I usually do two horizontal seams, one on each side of the center seam, then switch back to the vertical seams. Work out from the center, rerolling the quilt before each seam.

Quilt in the ditch between each border.

3. Clip the threads and remove the pins. If you added your borders traditionally, the quilt top is finished and ready for binding.

Otherwise, now is the time to add Quilt-As-You-Sew borders. Follow the directions in "Making the Weekend Quilt" on page 15.

Or if you are using the Modified Quilt-As-You-Sew borders, you do not need to cut separate strips of batting and border backing fabric. They are already included in your quilt.

Modified Quilt-As-You-Sew Borders

Instead of adding borders to the quilt and then layering and quilting as described previously, only the patchwork interior of the quilt is centered on the full-size backing and batting. After that section is quilted, quilt-as-you-sew borders are added to the quilt. They are added just as they would have been, except that you will sew through the batting and backing at the same time.

The point is, you have to make a seam to add the border to the quilt top center, why not quilt at the same time? Measure and cut the quilt borders. Unless I have a fabric or design that demands mitering, I find crossed or blunt borders to be just fine. Add the side borders first and then the ends, just as if you were adding borders before layering and quilting. When there are several borders, I prefer to add them one fabric at a time to create more quilting.

After the quilt interior is quilted, put it right side up on a large flat surface. Put the first side border right side down on top of the quilt just as if you were making a regular seam, **Fig H**. Pin in place. Stitch through all thicknesses, quilting and seaming at the same time. Repeat with the opposite side border. Open new borders flat into the proper position before adding borders on the ends of the quilt. Pin or very lightly press the first border flat before seaming across the end of it with another border.

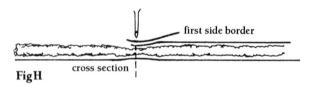

first side border

cross section

Fig H

Free Form Quilting Adds More Directions

Straight line quilting on the machine is really quite simple once you understand how to control the quilt and make it manageable. But what if you want to quilt in circles? Traditional sewing, where the feed dogs pull the fabric through the machine, would require somehow rotating that whole quilt around and through the machine. No way! So what happens if you disengage or lower the feed dogs? Well, basically, the needle goes up and down, but the machine doesn't move the fabric. That means you become the power moving the quilt under the needle and you can move it any direction you want, even in circles. The good part is you don't have to pivot the quilt around the needle!

That is why free form quilting is done with the feed dogs down. Most people like to replace the regular presser foot with the round embroidery or darning foot. When the presser foot is

42

lowered, the darning foot doesn't actually touch the fabric, but it identifies where the needle will be stitching and is a safety buffer for your fingers. Even if you decide to stitch without a presser foot of any kind, the lever for the presser foot must be lowered as that is the same action that controls the tension on the upper thread.

Free form means what it says. You can stitch any direction you want. The easiest free form quilting is done with random movements, like the border on the *Shaded Chevrons*. If you were going to try fancy feather quilting on the machine, this method is what you would use.

Keeping the fabric moving at a fairly calm steady pace and the needle moving fast seems to be the easiest way to keep your stitch length regular. The hardest thing to believe is that the faster you sew, the easier it is to do. Practice on a small piece of layered fabric, but remember, your stitch length will not have the same consistency as it does when the feed dogs and needle are completely synchronized.

The place you are most likely to get puckers in machine quilting is where two stitchings cross. A random motion that goes forward and curves back and cuts back again without actually crossing a previous stitching line will give you a nice quilted effect without puckers. Just a little practice and you'll be amazed at what you can do.

Use invisible thread or cotton thread that matches the major color in the fabric. There is less tension hassle with cotton thread. Remember to loosen your upper tension with the nylon thread. Your actual stitches are much less visible with the nylon thread.

Machine Quilting in Sections

While machine quilting techniques can be used on any size quilt, with larger quilts, there is a nice option for machine quilting a quilt in sections. In a nutshell, before completely sewing the patchwork interior together and adding the borders to the quilt, divide the quilt interior into quadrants. They don't have to be equal in size; they must have straight seams for combining later. At this point, your quilt will seem like four little crib quilts. Cut four backing pieces and four separate battings. Layer and machine quilt as described.

Put the quadrants together just like the individual blocks in the *Country Christmas Weekend Quilt*.

Now add borders in the original Quilt-As-You-Sew method used with the text quilt. Then bind as desired.

Flaps Add a Special Touch

A flap is just that. In sewing terminology, it might be described as piping without the cord. A flap is used when you need a tiny bit of color as an accent or to delineate. Just like an extra mat with a tiny edge of color may be the perfect accent when framing a pic-

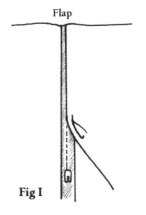

Flap

Fig I

ture, a flap can be the perfect touch for a quilt, **Fig I**. It can go between borders as on the *Mama Bear Linked Chevrons* or be used just before the binding.

While the flap looks like it is just tucked in between two layers of fabric when a seam is sewn, it isn't. It must be added separately just like a border and in the same order as the borders, or the corners won't overlap correctly.

The most common width of flap that I use is 1/4 inch. That means I cut a strip 1-inch wide on the straight grain. Fold and press it in half lengthwise. Line the raw edges of the flap up with the raw edges of the last section of quilt and stitch it in position. Then proceed with the next border or binding. Yes, the flap does encroach 1/4 inch onto the piece it is laying on, but I have never found it to be objectionable.

If you tried to insert a 1/4 inch border and were stitching down both sides, any deviation in the straightness of the seam would be very visible. This does not happen with flaps. Also the little bit of dimension that a flap gives is always very interesting.

Binding the Quilts
No Separate Binding

At least an inch of extra backing fabric must be allowed if it is your intention to finish a quilt this way. When finishing by bringing extra backing fabric to the front, the backing fabric must be selected to compliment the quilt. If I finish a quilt this way, I make sure that I stitch through the backing fabric to make the edge sturdier.

Separate Binding

The French fold binding is my favorite way to finish the edge of a quilt. It is cut four times as wide as the desired finished width PLUS 1/2 inch for two seam allowances AND 1/8 inch to 1/4 inch more to go around the thickness of the quilt. The fatter the batt, the more you need to allow here. Fold the binding strip in half lengthwise with the wrong sides together and the raw edges even. Press.

My favorite finished width is whatever size I think looks best on that quilt. Some quilts need a subtle narrow binding and others look best with a large, high contrast binding. The most common, however, is about 1/2 inch finished. With that width and an average full-size quilt, the equivalent of 5/8 yard of fabric is required for bindings alone. Just like borders, I prefer to cut the binding on the lengthwise grain and I avoid piecing whenever possible. If you don't want to piece the binding, the strips need to be cut from fabric as long as the quilt. There will, of course be lots of fabric left.

In my opinion, bias binding is only necessary if the edge is curvy. Some people believe that bias will wear longer, but I don't have evidence to that effect. Even if it is accurate, does that justify the extra time it takes to make bias?

Adding the Binding

After preparing the binding, prepare the quilt. Unless I have quilted very close to the edge of the quilt, I stabilize it before adding the binding. Machine baste 1/4 inch from the raw edge of the quilt top on all sides of the quilt before trimming away excess quilt batting and backing. Because I like full feeling bindings, I cut batting and backing almost, but not quite, twice as wide as the desired finished binding. When the binding is stitched onto the quilt and pulled flat onto the batting, it should be about 1/4 inch wider than the batting, **Fig J**.

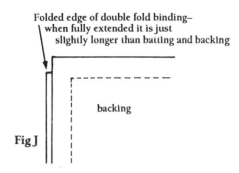

Folded edge of double fold binding–
when fully extended it is just
slightly longer than batting and backing

backing

Fig J

Lay binding on quilt so that both raw edges of binding match the raw edge of the quilt top and stitch in place. Roll binding around raw edge of quilt to the back and hand stitch in place using the row of machine stitching as a stabilizer and a guide, **Fig K**. Add binding strips in the same order as borders.

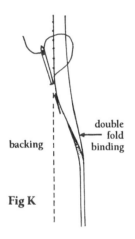

double
fold
binding

backing

Fig K

To make blunt corners (I feel mitered corners aren't necessary on most bindings), add bindings on sides of quilt first and complete the hand stitching. The hand hemming stitch I use is hidden. The needle comes out of the quilt and takes a bite of the binding and reenters the quilt exactly behind the stitch. The thread is carried in the layers of quilt, not on the outside. At corners, carefully stitch ends shut.

Measure quilt ends carefully. Add 1/2 inch at each binding end. To eliminate raw edges, turn them back to the wrong side before stitching in place.

At the corners, trim away enough batting and seam allowances to make the corners feel and look like the same thickness as the rest of the binding. Carefully stitch ends shut.

If you are hemming the binding by machine, attach binding to back and bring to front and either topstitch with invisible thread or experiment with your machine hemming stitch.

If You Must Piece the Binding
If you must piece the binding, flaps or borders, place the pieces at right angles and stitch diagonally as if you were piecing bias strips, **Fig L**. It eliminates bulk when the flaps and bindings are folded and the diagonal seams are less visible in a border.

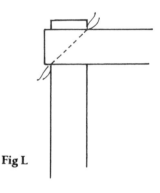

Fig L